Be Thou There

The Holy Family's Journey in Egypt

A National Egyptian Heritage Revival Book

Be Thou There

The Holy Family's Journey in Egypt

Edited with an introduction by
Gawdat Gabra

•

Text by
William Lyster
Cornelis Hulsman
Stephen J. Davis

•

Photographs by
Norbert Schiller

The American University in Cairo Press
Cairo • New York

Dedicated to the memory
of Metropolitan Athanasius,
Metropolitan of Beni Suef and Bahnasa (1923–2000)

Dar el Kutub No. 9225/00
ISBN 977 424 606 3

Norbert Schiller gratefully acknowledges the help and
support of the Associated Press and *Der Spiegel* magazine

Designed by the AUC Press Design Center/Andrea El-Akshar

Page ii: An old door leading
    into the Church of Saint John
    the Short at Dayr Abu Hinnis.

Page iv: The Worshiping Tree,
    near Gabal al-Tayr.

Pages vi–vii: Looking up at Gabal

Contents

Introduction

This book appears on the occasion of the two-thousand-year celebration of the Holy Family's flight into Egypt. The Gospel of Matthew tells us that the Lord appeared to Joseph in a dream and said to him, "Arise and take the young child and his mother, and flee into Egypt, and be thou there until I bring thee word: for Herod will seek the young child to destroy him" (Matt. 2:13). The Holy Scripture provides no information about the length of the sojourn of the Holy Family and the places they sought refuge in Egypt. This was left to tradition throughout the centuries. People sought an 'itinerary' of the Holy Family's journey in Egypt, which became a holy land, the only country that Jesus visited outside of Palestine. This book does not aim to supply such an itinerary or to verify the length of the Holy Family's stay in Egypt, but rather to present and assess the different sources and traditions that could be of interest to both the scholar and the general reader. In addition, this volume will document important monuments linked to the Holy Family, as well as how the tradition functions in Egypt today.

Egyptians were known to be a deeply religious people in ancient and medieval times. They continue to be religious, and many of their practices today can be traced to the ancient Egyptian culture. One of Egypt's most popular religious practices, both now and in the past, has been pilgrimage to sacred sites. In ancient times Abydos, Dendera, and Edfu were popular destinations. Festivals such as the procession of the god Amun from the temple of Karnak to the nearby temple of Luxor at Thebes linked neighboring shrines. Such festivals served also to link cults and shrines in far-flung places, as in the procession of the goddess Hathor from Dendera to the temple of Horus at Edfu in the southernmost part of Upper Egypt.

Festival processions of ancient Egyptian gods continued long after the spread of Christianity in Egypt; for example, the texts of the temple of Khnum at Esna show that public involvement in the pilgrimage circuits continued there as late as the third century, despite the fact that Christianity was already fairly well established in the region. The cult of the temple of Heliopolis continued at least until A.D. 360, and that of Isis survived in Philae as late as the sixth century, despite the presence of a Christian community since the fourth century. During the fifth century many pagan temples were Christianized and

In the Coptic Orthodox cemetery in Old Cairo.

churches were constructed within them—for example, at Abydos, Dendera, Thebes, Esna, and Aswan. The fifth century witnessed the replacement of the cult of Isis with the cult of Cyrus and John at the ancient pilgrimage site of Menuthis near Alexandria. Christian pilgrimage sites replaced pagan healing shrines. After the triumph of Christianity, some forms of popular entertainment, such as the theater and the circus, began to decline, while mass pilgrimages flourished. With the Arab conquest of Egypt, the church gradually became the major center of entertainment for Egyptian Christians, the Copts. The veneration shown by the Egyptians for pilgrimage sites is one of the most significant factors in the establishment of Christianity and its continuity in Egypt. Today, as in the past, the Copts boast that their land is blessed and protected because it gave refuge to the Holy Family, and they are proud to follow in the footsteps of Jesus in the Delta and in Upper Egypt.

The introductory chapter by William Lyster presents the story of the flight of the Holy Family in Egypt as it has developed in two thousand years. His approach to the history of Egyptian Christianity during Roman, Byzantine, and Muslim rule enables the reader to appreciate the ages during which the local traditions of the Holy Family's flight originated and developed. He touches on issues of early Christianity such as the Catechetical School of Alexandria, the Great Persecution (303–12), and the leading position of the patriarchs of Alexandria during the theological controversies of the fourth and the fifth centuries, especially concerning the doctrines of the Trinity and the Virgin Mary as the mother of God. In leading us to some of the pilgrimage sites associated with the Holy Family in Egypt, Lyster focuses on many aspects of the Coptic heritage and the achievements of the Copts, including monasticism, art, and architecture. This chapter also describes the Copts' social, economic, and political situations in different periods, which is essential for under-

standing the mentality of the Copts today, especially their present attitude toward the pilgrimage festivals related to the Holy Family. Lyster introduces all these elements for the first time in one harmonious context and invites the reader to learn about the Holy Family tradition in the context of a rich Coptic culture.

In the second chapter, we see how the traditions about the Holy Family remain very much alive today in Egypt. In a pioneering effort, Cornelis Hulsman conducted fieldwork all over Egypt. He has included in his work almost every place associated with the Holy Family and has visited even the sites that claim the blessings of the Holy Family despite the fact that they are not mentioned in any of the known sources. Some of the latter have found their way into the 'official itinerary'; others are only locally renowned. After interviewing bishops, priests, and many laypersons, Hulsman concludes that the traditions of the Holy Family in Egypt are vital to the psyche of the Copts. Even in the past two decades, new traditions have been added to the long chain of beliefs and pilgrimage sites. Faith in oral tradition is valued more than the literary evidence of the sources, and the apparitions and miracles play a crucial role in the rise and continuity of the traditions of the Holy Family's flight. Not only Christians seek the blessings of the Holy Family's pilgrimage sites, but also Muslims, who often go to the sites to seek healing for incurable diseases.

The last chapter, by Stephen Davis, investigates the ancient sources on the flight of the Holy Family into Egypt. Davis discusses the religious and historical significance of the sources in order to demonstrate their impact on the development of the traditions and the pilgrimage sites related to the Holy Family. He starts with the original story as it appears in the Gospel of Matthew, showing how the flight of the Holy Family was understood from the first as a fulfillment of biblical prophecy and how the land of Egypt was viewed as a place of refuge. The tradition of the Holy Family is the subject of interpretation and controversy in the writings of famous figures in early Christianity, such as Hippolytus of Rome, Origen of Alexandria, and Eusebius of Caesarea. Davis also points out that non-Christians heard about the flight into Egypt as early as the second century and that the tradition of three years and some months as the period of the sojourn of the Holy Family in Egypt dates to the early third century. By the fourth century, the oracle concerning Egypt—"Behold, the Lord rideth upon a swift cloud and shall come into Egypt" (Isa. 19:1)—was being interpreted as a prophecy of the Holy Family's flight.

Davis discusses extensively the roots of the local traditions, their development, the relationships among different localities in the tradition, and how a pilgrimage 'itinerary' of the Holy Family developed over the centuries. From Hermopolis (al-Ashmunayn), a site with a glorious history, arose the earliest local tradition about the Holy Family's route in Egypt. Many texts indicate that al-Ashmunayn is the origin of the 'itinerary' of the flight into Egypt; therefore, the sources on Hermopolis are discussed in great detail. It is not surprising that the two most important pilgrimage sites associated with Holy Family, Dayr al-Muharraq and Gabal at-Tayr, lie to the south and to the north, respectively, of Hermopolis.

In a new approach to the medieval sources, mainly in Arabic, Davis analyzes four categories of texts: homilies attributed to famous personalities of the Coptic Church, works on the history of the patriarchs of the Coptic Church and on the monasteries and churches in Egypt, liturgical books, and the so-called 'infancy gospels.' The study of these sources is very complex. For most of these sources, no precise date of authorship is available, and text-critical studies on the late medieval compilations are still in their beginnings. However, Davis shows the value of these sources and is able to trace their development. His innovative treatment of this material facilitates an appreciation of the tradition of the Holy Family in Egypt, one of the most important aspects of the Christian legacy in general and the Coptic Church in particular.

The great event of the flight of the Holy Family into Egypt continues to appeal to people's imagination. The traditions and the pilgrimage sites associated with the Holy Family in Egypt represent an important part of the Christian legacy in Egypt and throughout the world. With the increasing number of tourists visiting Egypt, the need for a book such as this is pressing. Our hope is that the educated layperson, the scholar, and the student will all benefit from its content. Norbert Schiller's exceptional skill in the photographic arts greatly enhances this valuable work.

I would like to thank Mark Linz, Neil Hewison, and their colleagues at the American University in Cairo Press for their invaluable help in producing this volume.

Gawdat Gabra
Director, Coptic Museum

من مصر
دعوت ابنى

Coptic Egypt and the Holy Family

William Lyster

Introduction

The Flight of the Holy Family into Egypt is mentioned only briefly in the Gospel of Matthew. Beyond that, we must look to the Coptic tradition for other information about their journey. Although this expanded tradition is largely based on written accounts, physical sites that have been popularly associated with the Holy Family also play an important role in supplying further details. Sites made sacred because they are believed to have been touched by the Holy Family often feature unusual physical manifestations. Some of these include miraculous hand- or foot-prints of the Christ Child, unusually shaped trees thought to have sheltered the Virgin, or healing springs where the family quenched their thirst. These sacred sites in turn find further material expression in architecture. Churches or monastic settlements mark most sites associated with the Holy Family in Egypt. The rich heritage of Coptic painting, in particular the production of icons and murals, is also an integral part of the network of belief and ritual practice shaped by the Coptic tradition of the Holy Family's journey in Egypt.

No specific architectural type is associated with the Holy Family sites in Egypt. Rather, the buildings at these sacred places are representative of various stages in the long span of Christian Egyptian architecture. The Coptic pictorial tradition, however, was conservative in nature. The iconographic image of the Flight has remained largely unchanged for the last fifteen hundred years. It shows the Virgin holding the infant Christ, riding a donkey, and Joseph on foot. In addition to the few depictions of the Flight that have survived from this long period, a much wider range of sacred images that do not at first appear to be closely tied to the journey of the Holy Family should actually be understood as making reference to it. Almost any depiction of the Virgin and Christ Child, a ubiquitous subject in Coptic art, can be seen as having points of connection with the Holy Family's trip, and with the transformation of Egypt into a second holy land.

The visual culture of the Holy Family's stay in Egypt has been in the making for almost two thousand years. It is a complex phenomenon, inextricably connected to the fabric of Coptic history and belief. A full appreciation of the Egyptian tradition of the Holy Family is possible only through an understanding of the long historical experience of the Copts. This chapter,

A modern Egyptian icon of the Flight. The Holy Family is shown traveling between the Nile and the Pyramids. Collection of the author (photo: Lyster).

therefore, will present the sites, buildings, and works of art associated with the Flight within a historical narrative of the Coptic people.

The Holy Family in Egypt

The story of the Holy Family's journey to Egypt is told in the second chapter of the Gospel of Matthew. When Jesus was born, Herod the Great (37–4 B.C.) was king of the Jews, as well as a client of the Roman emperor. Herod rebuilt the Temple in Jerusalem and founded the fortress of Masada, but he is chiefly remembered as propagator of the Massacre of the Innocents. According to Matthew, when the three wise men from the east informed Herod of the birth of a king in Bethlehem, he "sent forth and put to death all the male children in Bethlehem and in all its districts, from two years old and under" (Matt. 2:16). The Holy Family avoided the massacre by fleeing to Egypt, where they remained until an angel told Joseph that Herod had died.

Matthew is the only evangelist who mentions this story. He presents it as fulfillment of the words spoken by God to the prophet Hosea, "Out of Egypt have I called my son" (Hos. 11:1). Although Hosea was evoking Israel's special relationship with God through the memory of the Exodus, Matthew understood his words, eight hundred years later, as foretelling the coming of the messiah.[1] The use of quotations from the Old Testament to prove that Jesus was the fulfillment of the scriptures is characteristic of Matthew's gospel, and seems to have been common among the early Christians. Jesus himself predicted his death and his disciples' flight by quoting Zechariah 13:7 (Mark 14:27), while Paul writes that "Christ died for our sins according to the scriptures" (1 Cor. 15:3).[2]

Later generations of early Christians continued to look to the Old Testament for passages announcing the coming of Jesus. Eusebius of Caesarea (d. 339), the author of the first history of the early church, interpreted Isaiah 19:1 as a foretelling of the flight of the Holy Family, when "the idols of Egypt shall be moved at his presence."[3] Isaiah's prophecies were a politico-religious critique of the Kingdom of Judah in the eighth century B.C. He warned that an alliance against Assyria would be a covenant with death. Isaiah also foretold calamity for Egypt at the hands of God and the Assyrians (Isa. 19–20): the Egyptians would seek the comfort of their ancient religion in vain; the Lord would cause their idols to fall and destroy the council of their charmers, familiar spirits, and wizards. Yet, within his message of doom, Isaiah also offered hope to the land of the Nile. Out of the chaos of civil war and foreign conquest would come redemption. For God would not only smite Egypt, but heal it as well. Isaiah prophesied that the Egyptians would "cry unto the Lord because of the oppressors, and he shall send them a savior, and a great one, and he shall deliver them. And the Lord shall be known in Egypt, and the Egyptians shall know the Lord in that day" (Isa. 19:20–21). And God would say, "Blessed be Egypt my people" (Isa. 19:25). According to Christian tradition, the promise of Egypt's redemption was fulfilled by the visit of the Holy Family. When "the angel of the Lord appeareth to Joseph in a dream, saying Arise, and take the young child and his mother, and flee into Egypt" (Matt. 2:13), the Nile Valley became a part of the holy land.

Matthew records that the Holy Family remained in Egypt until Joseph was told of Herod's death in a dream. We are not told how long they stayed or given any geographic information about their journey; not even the Nile is mentioned. It was left to Coptic tradition to work out the details of the Holy Family's sojourn in Egypt. Information about their journey comes in two basic forms: written sources, which are examined by Stephen J. Davis in chapter 3, and physical manifestations, such as trees, caves, and springs that have somehow been touched by the passing of divinity. These sacred sites are scattered across the Delta, and are found along the Nile as far south as Asyut.

The fugitive Holy Family seems to have spent most of their time in Egypt traveling. Coptic icons of the Flight always show Mary, Jesus, and Joseph during their journey. Sometimes they are depicted in a boat on the Nile, but more often the Virgin and Christ Child ride a donkey and Joseph walks. Written accounts indicate that they received charity from pious strangers, but often they were without shelter, food, or water. Most of the sites associated with the Flight reflect some tribulation overcome by the Holy Family: walking in the heat of the day, they find shade under a tree, which is blessed; when they are hungry, a palm tree bows down, offering its dates; their thirst is quenched by local wells or, in more dire circumstances, by springs brought forth by the infant Jesus; while pursued by thieves, a tree opens up to hide them; and if there is no room in the inn, they sleep in a cave that miraculously appears.

After each encounter, the tree, well, or cave was endowed with miraculous healing power. In time, each became a place of pilgrimage that was marked by a church, monastery, or convent, usually dedicated to the Virgin Mary. The Copts have a long tradition of veneration of the Virgin. The Coptic liturgy proclaims, "Thou art exalted above the heaven and the most honored on the earth and of all creation therein, for thou didst become a Mother to the Creator."[4] Churches dedicated to al-'Adhrâ' (the Virgin) are found throughout Egypt. Most of them are not directly associated with the Flight, but their sheer number indicates the central position held by Mary in the devotions of the Copts. Six of the fifteen largest Christian *mulid*s (pilgrimage festivals) in Egypt are dedicated to the Virgin.[5] All but one are held at Holy Family sites. The exception is the *mulid* (April 2/Baramhat 24) at the Church of the Virgin at Zaytun in greater Cairo, where pilgrims celebrate the miraculous apparition of Mary in 1968 above the domes of the church.

A twentieth-century mosaic of the Virgin and Christ Child by Isaac Fanous in the Cathedral of St. Mark, Alexandria (photo: Lyster).

It is possible to chart the Holy Family's journey through Egypt by combining written sources with sacred geographical sites. A number of modern accounts have suggested such itineraries, while weaving the different legends into continuous narratives.[6] The Coptic Church has also recognized an official list of Holy Family sites for the bimillennial celebrations of the flight into Egypt.[7] These sites are examined in detail by Cornelis Hulsman in chapter 2, but an outline of the journey, as it is currently understood, will also be given here. The stages of the Holy Family's journey can be divided into four geographical groups: the coastal road linking Palestine to Egypt; the Nile Delta; the vicinity of greater Cairo; and the Nile Valley.

The Holy Family is believed to have traveled from Bethlehem to Gaza, where they took the coastal road into Egypt. Following in the footsteps of Abraham (Gen. 12:10), they passed through Pelusium (modern al-Farama) before entering Egypt at Bubastis (near Zagazig) in the eastern Nile Delta.[8] Both of these once-thriving cities are now abandoned ruins. The Holy Family's first visit to an Egyptian town was not encouraging. The entry into Bubastis (modern Tell Basta), sacred to the cat goddess Bastet, resulted in the collapse of the city's idols. The popular outcry against the strangers did not abate even when the infant Jesus miraculously brought forth a healing spring.[9] It was also in Bubastis that the Holy Family came to the attention of two thieves, an Egyptian and a Jew, who were to plague them for the rest of their stay in Egypt. A prophecy of the Christ Child identified the thieves as the two who would be crucified on Golgotha.[10]

Upon leaving Bubastis, the Holy Family traveled through the Delta. They crossed the Damietta (eastern) branch of the Nile at Samannud.[11] The modern church marking the site where they rested is dedicated to Apa Anub, a local fourth-century martyr. At Sakha, the infant Jesus left a footprint in stone before crossing the Rosetta (western) branch of the Nile.[12] Outside of Alexandria, the Holy Family turned south, avoiding the city altogether. While passing Wadi al-Natrun, a desert depression skirting the western Delta, the Christ Child foretold its later importance as a monastic center.[13]

The Holy Family then crossed the Nile near the future site of Cairo. They are believed to have returned to this area three years later when departing Egypt for Israel. A particularly large number of places in the vicinity of greater Cairo are linked to the Holy Family. The most important are presented here following a progression from north to south. At Musturud, northeast of the capital, the Christ Child brought forth a miraculous spring.[14] The site is also known as al-Mahamma, the place of the bath. A two-week *mulid* of the Virgin is celebrated here every August. In Matariya, near the modern suburb of Heliopolis, is the Virgin's Tree, an ancient sycamore that sheltered the Holy Family.[15] Harat Zuwayla is an active Coptic convent in the center of Cairo, and the medieval church there contains a spring blessed by Jesus.[16] Farther south is the Roman fortress of Babylon, the heart of Coptic Cairo. The Church of Abu Sarga, one of the oldest foundations in the fortress, features a crypt. Tradition has it that this subterranean space was originally a cave where the Holy Family found refuge.[17] In the southern suburb of Ma'adi, a church marks the spot where they set sail for Upper Egypt.[18]

The sources tell us that the first stage of the Holy Family's journey up the Nile was by boat. While traveling south on the river, a mountain peak at Gabal al-Tayr (near modern Samalut) bowed as the Christ Child passed. Jesus extended his hand and the mountain returned to its original position.[19] The ancient church at the peak of the cliff once contained the child's handprint miraculously preserved in stone. Amalric, the Crusader king of Jerusalem, is said to have hacked out and stolen the relic during his 1168 invasion of Egypt.[20] An important *mulid*

An icon by Anastasi al-Rumi (1849) from the Church of Abu Sarga, Old Cairo; the fortress of Babylon can be seen in the distance (drawing: Lyster).

of the Virgin is held at Gabal al-Tayr on the feast of her Dormition (January 29/Tuba 21).

Traveling again on land, the Holy Family proceeded south along the west bank of the Nile to Hermopolis Magna (modern al-Ashmunayn), probably the largest city they visited in Egypt.[21] Today, it is an archaeological site where two colossal stone-carved baboons sacred to the god Thoth stand guard next to the ruins of an impressive fifth-century Christian basilica. Hermopolis seems to have been the first site in Egypt identified with Isaiah's prophecy of the falling idols.[22] The miracle is said to have resulted in the governor adoring the Christ Child, and the conversion of the whole town. Such popular enthusiasm, however, did not encourage the Holy Family to settle in Hermopolis. After a short stay, they continued their journey, leaving behind a blessed tree and a miraculous handprint.

In Cusae, the Holy Family found a less welcoming response.[23] When pagan priests drove them from the city, the family found shelter in a small house in the neighboring countryside. Here they are said to have rested for six months until "an angel of the Lord appeared in a dream to Joseph in Egypt, saying, Arise, take the young child and his mother, and go to the land of Israel, for those who sought the young child's life are dead" (Matt. 2:19–20). The site of this 'second Bethlehem' is now occupied by Dayr al-Muharraq, one of the largest Coptic monasteries.[24] The stone altar in the Church of the Virgin there is believed to have been blessed twice, once by the Christ Child and again by a miraculous apparition after the Crucifixion. It is regarded as fulfillment of the prophecy of Isaiah, "In that day shall there be an altar to the Lord in the midst of the land of Egypt" (Isa. 19:19). Dayr al-Muharraq is the site of a *mulid* of the Virgin (June 28/Ba'una 21).

Another tradition says that the Holy Family ventured even farther south to Durunka, near Asyut, where they stayed in an ancient quarry.[25] In recent years, this cave at the top of a steep cliff has been transformed into the Monastery of the Blessed Virgin. Durunka is a major Coptic pilgrimage center. The twin feasts of the Virgin's Annunciation (August 13/Misra 7) and Assumption (August 22/Misra 16) are probably the largest Christian *mulid*s in Egypt.

Coptic Egypt

The medieval Coptic chronicler Abu al-Makarim (mistakenly identified as Abu Salih the Armenian) wrote a survey of the churches and monasteries of Egypt in the beginning of the thirteenth century. At that time, the Copts had lived under Islamic rule for more than five centuries, and were enjoying an era of relative peace and prosperity, despite previous periods of conflict. Abu al-Makarim describes hundreds of Christian sites throughout Egypt, many of which no longer survive. He remarks that the reason Egypt surpasses all other countries is "the sojourn in this land of our Lord Jesus Christ, in the flesh, with the Pure Lady Mary, and the truthful old man, Joseph the carpenter, by the command of God."[26] He then goes on to name numerous other biblical figures, from Abraham to Mark the Evangelist, whose presence in Egypt had also added to the country's excellence.

To this list of the blessed, Abu al-Makarim could have added an even larger number of local Christian saints, who were (and are) revered throughout the Nile Valley. The sacred geography of Christian Egypt is complex and dynamic. In addition to the sites associated with the Holy Family, there are many others linked to the apostles, martyrs, monks, patriarchs, and celestial beings named in the Coptic Synaxarium, the compilation of the lives of the saints. In every Coptic church are numerous icons, and usually more than one sanctuary, each dedicated to a different saint. At times, the array of Coptic saints encountered can be as confusing as the pantheon of the pharaohs.

Egypt was one of the first countries to con-

A nineteenth-century icon of the Flight in the Church of Abu Sarga, Old Cairo; the Holy Family is shown with their maidservant Salome.

vert to Christianity. The Coptic Church prides itself on being an apostolic foundation that has endured for nearly two thousand years. During most of this long period, the Christian Egyptians have been a subject people living under the control of Romans, Byzantines, Arabs, and Turks. The Copts were usually in religious opposition to the faith of Egypt's foreign rulers. As a result, Coptic art and architecture rarely received the benefit of imperial or royal support, so it lacks the monumental grandeur of ancient Egyptian temples or the mosques of medieval Cairo. But Coptic churches and monasteries, and the wall paintings and icons they contain, have a dignity and beauty all their own, which clearly indicates the faith and tenacity of the Coptic community. The sacred geography of Christian Egypt reflects not just the passing of the Holy Family, but the historical experience of the Copts.

Roman Egypt

When the Holy Family fled to Egypt a few years before Herod's death in 4 B.C., the country was a recently acquired province of the Roman Empire. It had been annexed by Octavian Caesar (later Emperor Augustus) in 30 B.C. following his victory over Cleopatra VII, the last of the country's Greek monarchs. Her family, the Ptolemies, had controlled Egypt since shortly after its conquest by Alexander the Great in 332 B.C. Under their rule, Alexandria, the Greek capital of Egypt, became the greatest city in the eastern Mediterranean. Famed for its lighthouse (one of the seven wonders of the world), the Museion, and library, it was a leading center of Greek learning and culture.

Alexandria also had the largest Jewish population outside of Palestine. Under the patronage of Ptolemy II (285–246 B.C.), the Torah was translated into Greek. The work is known as the Septuagint, after the seventy scholars involved in the project. Over the next century, the rest of the Hebrew scriptures were rendered into Greek. These later translations seem to have been primarily for the benefit of Alexandrian Jews who were no longer capable of reading Hebrew.[27] By the time of the Roman conquest, there had grown up in Alexandria a type of Judaism marked by a fusion of Jewish and Greek ideas. Philo Judaeus (d. A.D. 50), the Alexandrian philosopher, wrote in Greek about biblical stories, which he explained in Platonic and Stoic terms. The teachings of Philo had little impact on later Jewish tradition, but they were to influence profoundly the development of Christian theology. His allegorical approach to the Hebrew Bible was used to find prophecies of the New Testament.[28]

Traditional accounts indicate that the Holy Family never visited Alexandria. Instead, they spent three and a half years traveling among the Copts, the descendants of the ancient Egyptians. The name Copt derives from *Aigyptios*, Greek for 'Egyptian.' The Arabs pronounced this *Qibt*, which then passed into European languages as *Copt*. The name is currently used to describe Christian Egyptians who belong to the Orthodox Church of Egypt. At the beginning of the Christian era, most 'Copts' still worshiped the gods of the pharaohs and spoke Egyptian. This language was to become known as Coptic when written with Greek letters. Christianity is believed to have been brought to Egypt by Mark the Evangelist, who is regarded as the first in an unbroken line of 117 patriarchs of the Coptic Church. He began preaching the gospel in Alexandria during the reign of Emperor Claudius (A.D. 41–54). So great was the number of his converts that the pagans regarded him as a threat to the religious cults of the city. In A.D. 68, while celebrating Easter, Mark was killed by an infuriated mob. He thus became the first of the Egyptian martyrs.

The early history of the Church of Alexandria is obscure. The ten successors of Mark are known only by name. It is not until Demetrius I (189–231), the twelfth patriarch, that the sources supply some historical details. The Christian community at that time appears to have been large and comparatively wealthy. It possessed its own churches, as well as the most famous Christian school in the empire.[29] The Catechetical School of Alexandria was founded to instruct converts in the tenets of the faith. Pantaenus (ca.190), the first recorded head of the school, expanded the curriculum to include philosophy and the Greek humanities. Under Clement of Alexandria (d. 215) and Origen (d. 254), the Catechetical School became a rival of the pagan Museion as a center of learning in Alexandria. Both men were brilliant scholars who taught the Bible as the fulfillment of Greek philosophy. Their work prepared the way over the next century for the conversion of the Greek-speaking provincial aristocracy, which was fundamentally Platonist in outlook.[30]

The success of the church drew the wrath of the imperial authorities. Emperor Septimius Severus (193–211) launched the first coordinated persecution of Christians throughout the empire. Alexandria was particularly hard hit. Among the martyrs was Origen's father. The Severan persecution was the first great test of the Egyptian Christians. Their willingness to die for their faith ensured that the church emerged stronger from the ordeal.

The Coptic calendar is known as the 'Era of the Martyrs.' It begins in 284, the year that Diocletian (284–305) became emperor. In 303, he declared war on the church. The Great Persecution he unleashed was to last for nearly ten years. It began with the dismissal of Christians from the government and army. A later edict ordered everyone to offer sacrifice to the pagan gods on pain of death, an act Christians were not permitted to perform. The number of martyrs was legion. The most fero-

A Christian Egyptian police conscript touches an icon of the Flight, in the Church of the Holy Virgin at Ma'adi.

cious assault was directed against Egypt, where, according to the historian Eusebius, Christians formed the majority of the population.[31] He reports the deaths of thousands of Copts: "At times a hundred men would be slain in a single day along with women and children."[32]

The Coptic Synaxarium names 381 martyrs venerated by the Egyptian Church. Nearly half of these are stated to have suffered in the Great Persecution.[33] Saint Dimyana, to give but one example, was martyred in the eastern Delta at Bilqas, a site associated with the Holy Family.[34] She was the virtuous daughter of a Roman governor of Egypt. When Emperor Diocletian learned of her Christian faith, he sent a general and a battalion of soldiers to apprehend her. Having failed to persuade the saint to sacrifice to the pagan gods, they put her to torture. Dimyana was crushed, flayed, and boiled in oil, but after each agonizing ordeal God healed her and made her body whole. Finally, the saint won the crown of martyrdom when she was decapitated along with her forty virgin companions.[35] Dimyana and other Egyptian martyrs such as Menas, Mercurius, Apa Anub, and Theodore are still intensely venerated by modern Copts. Churches throughout Egypt are dedicated to these saints, and their sacred images are prominently displayed in Coptic homes and workplaces.

Byzantine Egypt

The conversion of Emperor Constantine (307–37) to Christianity brought an end to persecution. In 325, Constantine summoned the first Ecumenical Council at Nicea in Asia Minor to determine the relationship between the Father and the Son. The assembled bishops produced the Nicene Creed, in which Christ is stated to be "true God of true God, begotten not made, being of one substance with the Father. By whom all was made . . . in heaven and . . . on earth."[36] A contrary view, holding that the Son was less than the Father, was declared heretical, but later received the support of some of Constantine's successors. This so-called Arian heresy would divide the church throughout most of the fourth century.

Athanasius (326–73), the twentieth patriarch of Alexandria, was banished from his see by imperial order five times for refusing to deviate from the Nicene Creed. He was one of the greatest of the Greek theologians and successfully opposed emperors who held unorthodox views. The Alexandrian patriarch was also a great champion of the monastic movement. He spent his third exile (356–62) in a Coptic monastery in Upper Egypt, where he wrote the *Life of Saint Antony*, one of the most influential works of late antiquity. This text was instrumental in spreading Egyptian monastic practice to the rest of the Christian world. By winning the support of the monks, Athanasius united Greek- and Coptic-speaking Egyptians into a single church. A contemporary remarked that to be patriarch of Alexandria was to be king of the Christian world.[37]

The same year as the Council of Nicea, the sources tell us that Helena, the mother of Constantine, made a pilgrimage to the Holy Land, where she identified the caves associated with the Nativity in Bethlehem and the Holy Sepulchre in Jerusalem. Her son then constructed monumental churches at the sites she had indicated, thus establishing an imperial precedent for honoring places touched by members of the Holy Family. Constantine intended these churches to be basilicas "more beautiful than any on earth."[38]

The basilica was originally an all-purpose Roman building type, used for a whole range of functions. Constantine, wishing to give architectural expression to the new authority of the church, had the form adapted to the needs of Christian worship. The interior of a basilica is divided by rows of arcades into a central nave and two or more side aisles; the former is higher and wider than the latter. The buildings usually have pitched wooden roofs, and sometimes galleries are placed above the side aisles. After Constantine, the basilica became the most popular form of church architecture throughout the empire. The oldest surviving Egyptian churches are basilican in plan.[39]

Coptic churches, like most houses of Christian worship, are divided into two distinct areas, the nave and the sanctuary. The nave comprises the main body of the church, where the laity stand while attending the liturgy. The sanctuary, or *haykal*, is at the eastern end of the church. It is a small room containing a freestanding altar. Coptic churches usually have more than one *haykal*, each with its own dedication. According to canon law, a *haykal* may be used only once a day to celebrate mass, after which it must 'fast.' The sanctuary chambers are aligned side by side, often with connecting passages. One of the rooms may be used as a vestry, in which case it will not contain an altar. The sanctuary is separated from the nave by a continuous wooden screen, or *higab* ('veil'), that contains doors leading into the individual *haykal*s. The screen is usually surmounted by a row of icons, and lamps and ostrich eggs may also be suspended before the *higab*.

Two early Egyptian basilicas are located at sites associated with the Holy Family. The cathedral at Hermopolis (al-Ashmunayn), constructed between 430 and 440, must have been an impressive structure, indicative of the wealth and influence of the Egyptian church. Today, however, nothing survives but the foundations and a few upright columns. The Church of the Virgin at Gabal al-Tayr is said to have been founded in 328 by Empress Helena. Such an early date is unlikely, but the building appears to be of considerable antiquity. It stands on a cliff known as the Mountain of the Birds (Gabal al-Tayr), more than a hundred meters above the Nile. The church is hewn out of limestone. Twelve rock-cut columns support arcades surrounding a square nave. Stone benches cut into the walls of the narthex (west) and two side aisles (north and

south) suggest that the church was used as a healing shrine. Pilgrims may have spent the night on the benches in the hopes of receiving a dream cure from the Virgin. Between the nave and the sanctuary is a *khurus* (choir), the chamber in Coptic churches that separates the congregation from the altar. This additional space, reserved for priests, seems to have been adopted in the seventh century, but its use eventually fell out of practice in the late medieval period.[40] To the south of the central *haykal* is a small cave dedicated to the Virgin. The upper galleries and the domes of the church were added in 1933.

An interesting modern practice, which likely has roots in the distant past, is performed by newly married couples at Gabal al-Tayr. They paint crosses with henna inside the church, in hopes of bearing children. While this practice has not, to my knowledge, been studied, it seems likely that it is carried out at this site specifically because the Holy Family spent time there. The birth and safety of the Christ Child would ensure the fertility of the new wife and the health of the couple's child.

Gabal al-Tayr once belonged to a Coptic monastery dedicated to the Virgin, although that community no longer exists. The monastery's location on top of the limestone ridge made access very difficult. Visitors were hauled up the cliff face in a hoop secured by rope netting. The monastery was popularly known as Dayr al-Bakkara ('the monastery of the pulley'). Many Holy Family sites in Egypt are marked by monastic communities, including those at Durunka (Asyut), Dayr al-Muharraq (al-Qusiya), Ma'adi (Cairo), Harat Zuwayla (Cairo), and Wadi al-Natrun (between Cairo and Alexandria).

In the fourth century, as Christianity emerged as the official religion of the Roman Empire, the number of monasteries in Egypt grew at a phenomenal rate. Thousands of men and women abandoned the world for a life of the spirit, until "the desert grew full of monks."[41] Antony the

The Galaktotrophousa (Nursing Virgin) in a painted apse from the Monastery of Apa Jeremias at Saqqara (circa sixth century), Coptic Museum, Cairo. After J. E. Quibell (photo: Lyster).

Great (d. 356), the father of Christian monasticism, was born to a prosperous peasant family in Upper Egypt. While still a young man, he followed the advice of Jesus literally: "If thou wilt be perfect, go and sell that thou hast, and give to the poor, . . . and come and follow me" (Matt. 19:21). For nearly eighty years he resided in the desert practicing what became known as the 'angelic life,' a quest for spiritual perfection. During the worst phase of the Great Persecution, Antony left the desert for Alexandria. As Athanasius records, "He longed for martyrdom, but the Lord was keeping him that he might teach many the practice of asceticism that he had learned from the scriptures. Many merely on seeing him were eager to imitate his manner of life."[42]

Antony had many imitators. Monasteries for men and others for women were built outside of practically every town and village in Egypt. More determined monks, following Antony's example, moved to the desert. Around 320, Ammon (d. 353) settled in the desert of Nitria, west of the Nile Delta. Soon five thousand monks were living at Nitria, each in a separate cell. The desert grew so crowded that Ammon, following the advice of Antony, established a second community, known as Kellia ('Cells'), deeper in the desert. It served as a place of greater solitude for more experienced monks. By the end of the fourth century, there were as many as six hundred monks at Kellia.[43]

At the same time, Macarius the Great (d. 390) established a community at Scetis, the ancient name for Wadi al-Natrun. Accounts of his life tell us that he was directed to the site by a cherub. Macarius founded the monastic settlement that bears his name (Dayr Abu Maqar), and established a second community called Dayr al-Baramus ('monastery of the Romans') in honor of two young men from Constantinople who had become monks and died in the desert. Wadi al-Natrun is associated with many famous desert fathers. Pishoi, now commonly called Bishoi, founded the

monastery that now serves as the papal monastic residence. A century later, monks from the Monastery of Bishoi established the neighboring Dayr al-Suryan dedicated to the Virgin.[44] This region, which is still an active monastic center, is believed to have been blessed by the infant Jesus during the flight of Holy Family.

Early Coptic monks lived in caves and small huts that were isolated from each other in the desert. They followed an *abba* ('father'), who was a more experienced monk. He instructed them in spiritual discipline and survival in the desert. The threat of nomads, who periodically plundered monastic settlements, compelled monks to form tighter communities. During the ninth century many monasteries of Egypt were fortified for reasons of security.

In the Byzantine period, churches were commonly decorated with wall paintings. Unfortunately, very few examples have been preserved. One of the earliest to survive is the rock-cut church at Dayr Abu Hinnis, near al-Shaykh 'Ibada, across the river from Ashmunayn. It was probably constructed in the fifth century as a shrine to Colluthus, a local healing saint martyred in the Great Persecution. The martyrium in time attracted Christian hermits, who dug cells around the church on the slope of the eastern desert plateau. Today, the caves and ruined church are an archeological site. Nearby, an ancient basilica still serves as the village church.[45]

Dayr Abu Hinnis is also on the route that the faithful believe was taken by the Holy Family to Upper Egypt. It is appropriate, therefore, that the small cave church contains one of the earliest known depictions of the Flight in Christian art. The main room of the building seems to have been painted in the fifth century with episodes from the life of Christ.[46] Only scenes of his infancy are partially preserved in the northeastern corner of the church. They form a continuous frieze occupying the upper half of the walls. Herod is shown enthroned in a palace. Next to him, three soldiers carry out the Massacre of the

Innocents, while an angel warns a sleeping Joseph of approaching danger. The last surviving panel is of the Flight. Although the painting is severely damaged, it can still be determined that the image is consistent with what later became the conventional depiction of the subject.[47] At Dayr Abu Hinnis, Joseph is shown walking along side the Virgin, who is mounted on a donkey while holding the Christ Child. Behind the Holy Family is a tree indicating an outdoor setting. The tree may have been a palm, and as such was probably intended as a reference to the Entry into Jerusalem, an iconographic subject which shares many similarities with that of the Flight.[48] Most of the early Coptic paintings known to us were discovered in the course of archeological excavations. They usually came from the oratories (chapels) of monastic settlements, and are usually dated tentatively to the sixth and seventh centuries. The walls of the chapels were painted with images of Christ, the Virgin, martyrs, monks, and biblical scenes.

An apse at the center of the eastern wall of these early oratories was the main focus of both devotion and decoration. A number of painted apses from this period are on display in the Coptic Museum in Cairo. They are often divided into two painted registers, where Christ Pantocrator ('ruler of all') fills the hood of the apse above a lower level of saints arranged around its inner curve. A celebrated example from Bawit has a lower register featuring an enthroned Virgin with the Christ Child on her lap, flanked by the standing Apostles and two local saints.[49]

In a painted apse from the Monastery of Apa Jeremias at Saqqara, the hood of the niche contains a bust of Christ in a circular *mandorla* (body halo). The lower zone features an enthroned Virgin, protected by the archangels Michael and Gabriel. The Christ Child is shown as a smaller version of the Pantocrator seen above. He is set within a circular medallion (*clipeus*) placed over the bosom of the Virgin.[50]

The iconographic image symbolizes the Incarnation of the eternal Word of God, while emphasizing that Mary is the Theotokos ('God-bearer').[51] The Virgin is addressed in the Coptic liturgy as "the high Tower in which is found the honorable jewel that is Emmanuel, who came and dwelt in thy womb. So we honor the virginity of the Bride, uncorrupted, pure, and holy, the God-Bearer, Mary."[52] The Virgin's role as mother of God is stressed in another painted apse from Saqqara, where she is shown suckling the Christ Child. The Galaktotrophousa ('nursing Virgin'), accompanied by two angels, fills the entire niche.[53]

Devotion to the Virgin Mary as Theotokos is characteristic of Coptic Christianity. Cyril (412-44), the twenty-fourth Patriarch of Alexandria, placed himself at the center of a new theological controversy by emphasizing the divinity of Christ and the Virgin's role as mother of God. The rival patriarchal sees of Constantinople and Antioch stressed the humanity of Jesus. Nestorius, the patriarch of Constantinople, taught that Jesus was born a man who received the Holy Spirit only at the time of his baptism. He also denied Mary the title of Theotokos. In his interpretation, she was the bearer of the messiah, but not the mother of God. The theological argument was primarily concerned with nature of Christ, but the veneration of the Theotokos rallied the Egyptians behind their patriarch. At the Council of Ephesus in 431, Cyril's definition

The wall painting of Joseph's Dream and the Flight (circa fifth century) from Dayr Abu Hinnis. After Nicole Thierry (drawing: Lyster).

of the nature of Christ's person was accepted as orthodox. The prestige of the patriarch of Alexandria had never been greater.[54]

Dioscurus (444–54), the twenty-fifth patriarch, lacked the diplomatic skills of his illustrious predecessors. He upheld the teachings of Athanasius and Cyril that Christ has two natures—divine and human—mystically united in one, without confusion, corruption, or change.[55] His opponents held that the human and divine natures of Christ remained separate. At the second Council of Ephesus in 449, Dioscurus' guard of desert monks used violence to silence all opposition. In the aftermath of this 'Robber Council,' the patriarchal sees of Rome, Constantinople, and Antioch united to break the power of Alexandria. Two years later, in 451, the Council of Chalcedon deposed Dioscurus and declared his position on the nature of Christ heretical. The teachings of Athanasius and Cyril, however, were accepted as orthodox. The council also affirmed the primacy of Constantinople in the Eastern Church. The emperor appointed a patriarch to the see of Saint Mark, who was loyal to the tenets of Chalcedon. The Copts rejected his authority and elected a pope of their own. Meanwhile, the churches of Syria, Armenia, and Ethiopia also adopted Alexandria's monophysite (one nature) position. The religious unity of the Eastern Christian world had been sundered.[56]

Over the next century, both sides sought a compromise. The theological debate probably could have been resolved, but the political and personal issues were insurmountable. Neither Alexandria nor Constantinople would give ground on the question of primacy. The posthumous reputation of Dioscurus was equally divisive. He was a saint to the Egyptians, but the supporters of Chalcedon regarded him as a villain. By the reign of Justinian (527–65), imperial attitudes toward the Copts had hardened, and the Egyptian Church once again faced persecution.[57] The Copts established a rival church

hierarchy, refusing communion with the Chalcedon party, as did their monophysite brethren in Syria, who became known as 'Jacobites.'[58] The monasteries of Egypt were strongholds of Coptic orthodoxy and the focus of popular devotion. They supplied most of the higher clergy of the church. Under Peter IV (567–69), the thirty-fourth patriarch, there were "six hundred flourishing monasteries, like beehives in their populousness."[59] The force of imperial arms maintained a Chalcedonian clergy in Egypt. They controlled the largest churches, such as the basilica of Hermopolis, but did not command the loyalty of the Egyptian people.

Egypt under Islamic Rule

The Arab conquest brought to an end nearly seven hundred years of Romano-Byzantine rule in Egypt. In 641, the Arabs captured the Roman fortress of Babylon at the strategic point where the Nile Valley meets the Delta. Later the same year, the Byzantine governor surrendered Alexandria before evacuating Egypt with his army and entourage. The Arabs then founded a garrison town to the north of Babylon named al-Fustat, which would eventually grow into the great city of Cairo.

The Arabs had no experience managing the agricultural production upon which the wealth of Egypt was based. They adopted the Byzantine system of taxation and left it in the hands of the Copts, who were to staff the Muslim fiscal administration for centuries. The Copts cooperated with their new Arab masters, as they had with the equally unsympathetic Byzantine government. The Arabs classified the Copts as *ahl al-dhimma*, a 'protected people,' whose faith was to be respected. Christians and Jews were 'people of the book,' the recipients of scripture from the same divine force that inspired the Quran. As protected subjects, the Copts were granted personal security, freedom of religion, and a degree of autonomy in the conduct of their communal affairs. They were also obliged to pay an additional poll tax and accept certain legal and social restrictions. Christians were prevented from building or repairing churches, displaying crosses or holy books in public, or converting anyone to their faith. As a subject people, they were forbidden to bear arms, ride horses, or have houses taller than those of the Muslims.[60]

Positions of influence in the Egyptian administration enabled the Copts to win concessions from Muslim rulers that often violated the strict terms imposed after the conquest. The Arab governor 'Abd al-'Aziz ibn Marwan (d. 704) was the virtual viceroy of Egypt for nearly twenty years. He was a leading member of the Umayyad family that ruled the Islamic Empire between 661 and 750. The governor's Coptic secretary, Athanasius, was granted permission to build churches within the confines of the fortress of Babylon, which had become a Coptic quarter after the Arab conquest. Among the churches erected by Athanasius was one dedicated to Saint Sergius (Abu Sarga), a soldier martyred under Diocletian. The building served as the cathedral of the local bishop, and is also an important Holy Family site.

During the first two centuries of Arab rule, Egypt was a wealthy but not particularly influential province of the Islamic Empire. Under the 'Abbasid caliphs of Baghdad (750–969), governors of Egypt rarely ruled for more than a few years. Their sole concern was a high tax yield, regardless of the consequences for the country. In the eighth and ninth centuries, heavy taxation sparked revolts among the Coptic peasantry of the Delta. Early uprisings at Samannud and Sakha, both sites associated with the Holy Family, were easily suppressed.[61]

The Bashmuric rebellion of 829–32 was a more serious threat to Arab rule. The Coptic rebels, centered in the marshlands of the lower Delta, successfully resisted an 'Abbasid expeditionary force sent from Baghdad, until Caliph al-Ma'mun (813–33) was obliged to take personal command of the operation. The revolt was brutally crushed. According to the fifteenth-century historian al-Maqrizi, the failure of the Bashmuric rebellion resulted in the conversion to Islam of most of the Coptic population of the Delta.[62] For the first time, Muslims were the majority population in the Nile Valley. It was a decisive step in the transformation of Egypt into a predominantly Muslim country.

After the suppression of the Bashmuric rebellion, the 'Abbasid caliphs entrusted the administration of Egypt to Turkish and other non-Arab soldiers. Two of these military governors, Ahmad ibn Tulun (868–84) and Muhammad ibn Tughj al-Ikhshid (935–46), managed to establish short-lived dynasties. Their families ruled Egypt as autonomous, hereditary governors, but never questioned the ultimate sovereignty of the 'Abbasid caliph, the commander of all Sunni Muslims. The Fatimid caliphs of North Africa, however, rejected all 'Abbasid authority. They were the direct descendants of the Prophet Muhammad and the divinely inspired *imams* (spiritual leaders) of the Isma'ilis, a Shi'i sect with adherents throughout the Islamic world. The Fatimids regarded the 'Abbasids as usurpers of their rightful position as leaders of the Muslim community. In 969, they conquered Egypt and established Cairo as the center of their independent caliphate. Under the Fatimids, Egypt achieved a position of preeminence in the Muslim world that it has retained until today.

The Fatimid caliphs (969–1171) ruled as a religious minority. Their Egyptian subjects were predominantly Sunni Muslims and Coptic Christians, but there were smaller communities of other Christian sects and Jews. The caliphs made little effort to convert their subjects to Shi'ism, and members of all faiths held positions of authority in their government. Coptic officials enjoyed exceptional prominence. Their main area of competence was as tax collectors and scribes in the civil service, but particularly capable individuals could rise to positions of even greater authority. 'Isa ibn Nasturus was appointed *wazir*, the highest office of state, by Caliph al-'Aziz (975–96). Other Copts served in more personal capacities at the Fatimid court. The secretary of Caliph al-Hafiz (1131–49) was a Copt, as were his doctor and astrologer.[63]

The religious leaders of Egypt, including the Coptic patriarch, the chief Sunni *qadi* (judge), and the head rabbi, were always present in attendance on the caliph or his *wazir*. They protected the interests of their communities, while serving as guarantors of their people's loyalty. In 1070, the sixty-sixth Coptic patriarch Christodoulos (1047–77) relocated the papal seat from Alexandria to Cairo in order to be closer to the center of power.[64] The Fatimids staged disputations between the rival faiths and rewarded the most successful arguments. Sawirus ibn al-Muqaffa', bishop of al-Ashmunayn (d. ca. 979) "disputed many times with the *qadi*s of the Muslims by the order of Caliph al-Mu'izz (953–75), and he overcame them through the power of God and His grace."[65]

Bishop Sawirus held his own in the polemics at the Fatimid court thanks to his "grace and power in the Arabic tongue . . . bestowed upon him by God." He was also a prolific writer in Arabic and is credited with the composition of thirty-eight works of theology, history, and science.[66] His most famous book, *The History of the Patriarchs of Alexandria*, was translated from Greek and Coptic sources and was added to until the early twentieth century by subsequent authors. Christian Arabic literature, both translations of Coptic texts and original compositions in Arabic, flourished under the Fatimids. In time, Arabic eclipsed the writing of Coptic in Egypt. Efforts were taken to preserve the language through the compilation of Coptic-Arabic dictionaries, but the last substantial Coptic literary work dates from the fourteenth century.[67]

Displays of royal favor toward the Copts were not always popular among the Muslims of Egypt. Caliph al-Mu'izz granted the sixty-second Coptic patriarch Ibrahim ibn Za'rah (975–78) permission to rebuild the Church of Saint Mercurius in the vicinity of the main congregational mosque of Old Cairo. Public demonstrations prevented the work from commencing until the caliph personally intervened with his troops and dispersed the hostile crowd.[68] Similar protests occurred throughout the medieval period. They were usually the result of popular Muslim resentment that the Copts had obtained positions of undue authority and influence. The Fatimids occasionally bowed to public pressure by dismissing Christian officials and reviving discriminatory restrictions, such as the prohibition of riding horses and the requirement that all Copts wear blue turbans to distinguish them from the Muslims, who wore white.[69] Ironically, these periods of repression are often an indicator of the success of the Copts within Muslim society. The persecution by Caliph al-Hakim (996–1021) seems to have been a violent reaction to the favor shown to the Copts by his father, al-'Aziz. In 1138, Ridwan ibn al-Walakhshi, the Sunni Muslim *wazir* of Caliph al-Hafiz, removed Coptic officials and renewed the usual sumptuary laws. Ridwan had come to power by overthrowing his predecessor, a Christian Armenian. His persecution of non-Muslims was used to consolidate his position and win popular support. It quickly subsided once the *wazir* had achieved his objectives.[70]

Salah al-Din ibn Ayyub, the founder of the Ayyubid dynasty (1171–1250), reintroduced Sunni Islam as the official faith of Egypt. He came from a Kurdish military family that had risen to prominence in the Muslim struggle against the Crusaders. In 1187, Salah al-Din crushed the Crusader army and captured Jerusalem. The Christian response was the Third Crusade, the legendary confrontation between Salah al-Din and Richard the Lion-Hearted of England. The Crusaders regained control of the eastern Mediterranean coast, but failed to conquer Jerusalem. On the death of Salah al-Din in 1193, his family controlled Egypt, Syria, and portions of modern Iraq and Turkey.[71]

Salah al-Din had built an empire through the propagation of holy war. His Ayyubid successors tried to maintain their inheritance by avoiding military conflicts with the Crusaders.[72] Sultan al-Kamil (1228–38), the nephew of Salah al-Din, ruled Egypt for almost forty years, first as governor for his father al-'Adil (1200–18), then as sultan in his own right. He was a tolerant monarch who, according to the *History of the Patriarchs*, "extended justice to his subjects, and dispensed goodness to them; and they were days of abundance and many good things."[73]

Under the Fatimid caliphs and Ayyubid sultans, the Copts experienced a long period of relative peace and security. They formed a tightly knit community under the direction of their patriarch and higher clergy. Copt officials had access to positions of authority in the Muslim government and were able to protect the interests of their people. During the Fatimid period in particular, the Coptic Church enjoyed an increase in its revenues.[74] This medieval era of prosperity also witnessed the construction of churches throughout the country. The chronicler Abu al-Makarim mentions more than six hundred Coptic churches active at the beginning of the thirteenth century.[75] Most of the churches of Old Cairo were founded or restored at this time, including those associated with the Holy Family.

Medieval Coptic churches generally present an unimposing exterior. They rarely have bell towers or exterior decoration, and the entrances are often through small side doors. The Copts may have prospered under the Fatimids and the Ayyubids, but they remained a subject people. In times of political disorder or popular unrest, they were exposed to persecution and outbreaks of sectarian violence. Coptic churches were fre-

quently pillaged or destroyed during anti-Christian riots. Over the centuries, they were restored or rebuilt numerous times. Each renovation would introduce new materials, as well as incorporate older elements, such as columns, capitals, and lintels, taken from earlier structures. The churches also received periodic pious donations from Coptic notables, including new sanctuary screens, pulpits, and icons. As a result, it is often difficult to assign precise dates to these buildings. The Church of Abu Sarga in Babylon, one of the most important of the Holy Family sites in the region of greater Cairo, for example, was first erected around 685. It was restored in the eighth century, then rebuilt in 1171 after the church was partially burned during the chaotic last days of Fatimid rule. Since then it seems to have been restored and parts of it rebuilt a number of times.

Within Abu Sarga, the architectural form and elements are a mixture of the ancient, the medieval, and the modern. The basic form of the church is basilican, and it is therefore a descendant of the major Christian structures commissioned by Emperor Constantine at Jerusalem and Bethlehem. One of the most important modifications introduced into Coptic architecture during the medieval period was the use of domes. The Copts had employed domes and vaults in their churches before the Arab conquest, but it was only after the Fatimids began using domes as a major component of their public buildings that they were widely adopted by the Copts. At first, domes were placed over the sanctuaries of earlier basilican-style churches, where wooden roofs covered most of the interior. In the Church of Abu Sarga, vaulted wooden roofs cover the nave and central sanctuary, but a large dome was erected in 1171 over the northern *haykal*. Gradually, multiple brick domes began to replace the timber roofs of Coptic churches throughout Egypt. Domes created impressive interior spaces at a fraction of the cost of wooden roofs, and

offered greater protection against fire. Three domes cover the Church of the Virgin at Ma'adi, where the Holy Family is believed to have set sail for Upper Egypt. The Church of the Virgin in Dayr al-Muharraq, built on the site where the Holy Family lived for six months, has nine domes above the nave. In some Coptic churches brick vaults are also used in conjunction with domes. The Church of the Holy Virgin at Sakha, the site of a miraculous footprint of the Christ Child, has domes over its three sanctuaries, but a large barrel vault of brick surmounts the nave. The use of domes and vaults was to remain a notable feature of Coptic architecture throughout out the medieval and modern periods. Today, domes and vaults cover most Coptic churches.

Returning to the Church of Abu Sarga, the architectural elements of the interior show a similar mixture of historical periods. The wooden altar, now in the Coptic Museum, dates from before the Arab conquest, as do the marble columns and capitals supporting the medieval arcades of the nave.[76] The inlaid wooden screen of the central sanctuary includes carved panels, probably from the thirteenth century, depicting saints and biblical scenes. The screens of the side sanctuaries are dated to 1738. Most of the icons in the church are also from the eighteenth century. The marble pulpit supported by ten columns is a modern copy of the *ambon* (pulpit) in the Church of Saint Barbara.[77]

The tradition of Coptic religious painting has its origins in late antiquity, but it appears to have continued throughout the medieval period. While Coptic churches were painted in earlier centuries, the best preserved examples were produced between the eleventh and fourteenth centuries. Surviving paintings are often undated, which has given rise to a fair amount of scholarly controversy. Among the best-preserved from the medieval period in Egypt are those in the Church of the Virgin at Dayr al-Suryan in Wadi al-Natrun. The church is of special interest because it contains a particularly large number of paintings depicting scenes from the life of the

Virgin and the infancy of Christ, very possibly in response to the traditional belief that the infant Jesus foretold the future prominence of the area as a center of monasticism.

Dayr al-Suryan ('monastery of the Syrians') was founded in the early sixth century by a group of Coptic monks from the neighboring Dayr Anba Bishoi, who dedicated it to the Virgin Mary. A century or two later, Syrian Jacobites acquired the monastery from the Coptic patriarch as a permanent home for their monks in Wadi al-Natrun. It remained in Syrian hands until the late seventeenth century, but was often shared with Coptic monks.[78] Dayr al-Suryan is now a Coptic Orthodox monastery.

The Church of the Virgin, founded around 645, has three distinct levels of paintings.[79] The earliest are non-figural motifs, such as crosses, painted in ocher. They were covered in plaster at a later date, and a new painted program was added to the church. This second stage seems to have also involved structural modifications to the church, including the building of a semi-dome at the western end of the nave.[80] In this vault was painted a magnificent Annunciation, one of the masterpieces of medieval Egyptian painting. At the center of the composition, a seated Virgin is approached by the archangel Gabriel. The pair is flanked by Isaiah and Moses on the right and Ezekiel and Daniel on the left. Each of the Old Testament figures holds a scroll upon which is written in Coptic a prophecy of the Immaculate Conception.[81] Around 1225, this Annunciation was plastered over and replaced by a new painting of the Ascension containing inscriptions in Syriac. It was only revealed in 1991, when the plaster level of the later painting was removed after being damaged by a fire.[82] Suggested dates for the painting of the Annunciation have ranged from the eighth to the late twelfth century.[83] This span of four hundred years gives some indication of the difficulties in dating Coptic medieval paintings.

The two painted semi-domes in the *khurus* are also part of the third 'Syriac' program from the early thirteenth century. The northern vault is divided between a new Annunciation and a Nativity, while the southern semi-dome features the Dormition of the Virgin.[84] It is not known whether the painters were Copts or Syrians. Recent conservation work in the church has uncovered other paintings, including an image of the nursing Virgin (Galaktotrophousa) on the southern column near to the entrance of the central sanctuary. The date of this painting is uncertain, but it may be contemporary with the earlier Annunciation.[85]

Medieval Coptic painters seem to have been professionals who were willing to travel great distances to accept commissions. Painted churches are found in Cairo, Wadi al-Natrun, the Fayyum,

The Galaktotrophousa (circa seventh to tenth century) painted on a column in the Church of the Virgin, Dayr al-Suryan (photo: Lyster).

Upper Egypt, and by the Red Sea. It is likely that the same painters also produced icons and illuminated manuscripts to supplement their income.[86] Unfortunately, almost no Coptic icons have been identified as belonging to this period, but a number of manuscripts survive. The Institut Catholique in Paris has a Gospel manuscript written in Coptic and Arabic that was produced in Cairo in 1250.[87] It contains eighteen pages of miniature paintings, most of which are divided into squares containing different scenes from the life of Jesus. The paintings are a fascinating blend of Christian and Muslim styles. Jesus and his disciples wear biblical costumes and are placed against a golden background in a traditionally Byzantine manner, but other elements are drawn from contemporary Muslim society. Figures are depicted wearing turbans and seated cross-legged in Arab fashion, and soldiers are shown in military garb of the period. Arabesques and geometric patterns are used as borders and decorative details.

Three painted scenes from the Gospel of Matthew concern the flight into Egypt.[88] They are grouped together at the top of the same page, forming a mini-narrative. An enthroned

A miniature of the Flight (1250) from a Copto-Arabic New Testament made in Cairo (drawing: Lyster).

Herod is shown meeting the three Magi on horseback. The next square depicts the Flight, one of the only Coptic examples of this subject from the medieval period. Mary holds the Christ Child while riding a white donkey. Joseph follows behind with their maidservant Salome, who according to Coptic tradition accompanied the Holy Family into Egypt. The final picture of the group is of the Massacre of the Innocents.

In the same year that this manuscript was produced, the Turkish *mamluk*s (military slaves) of the last Ayyubid sultan assassinated their master and seized control of Egypt. Under the rule of the Bahri Mamluks (1250–1382), the position of the Copts deteriorated rapidly. Official discrimination was more consistently applied, while outbreaks of popular sectarian violence became more common. The first indication of the changing status of *dhimmi*s of Egypt occurred during the second reign of Sultan al-Nasir Muhammad (1299–1309). Christians and Jews were dismissed from the government and ordered to fulfill the conditions that had been imposed on them following the Arab conquest. The historian al-Maqrizi explains that this "misfortune befell the people of the protected religions . . . because they lived a life of increasing luxury in Cairo and Fustat and indulged in such things as riding on fine horses and splendid mules with magnificent trappings, and wore sumptuous clothes, and received high positions." Al-Maqrizi also notes that when the decree of the sultan became known to the Muslim common people, "they turned on the Christians and destroyed two of their churches. They also destroyed Jewish and Christian houses that overtopped the houses of their Muslim neighbors."[89]

During the reign of Sultan al-Salih (1351–54), riots again broke out in response to the wealth and influence of the Copts. More churches in Cairo were destroyed, and Christian officials were attacked on the street. The discriminatory measures promulgated in 1301 were reissued. In addition, most of the land in Egypt owned by churches and monasteries, amounting to 25,000 *feddan*s, was confiscated, effectively breaking the economic power of Christian institutions in Egypt.[90] Al-Maqrizi explicitly states that conversion now took place on a wide scale. "In all the provinces of Egypt, both north and south, no church remained that had not been razed; on many of those sites mosques were constructed. For when the Christians' affliction grew great and their income small, they decided to embrace Islam. Thus Islam spread among the Christians . . . . This was a momentous event in Egyptian history. From that time on lineages became mixed."[91]

Official oppression, the destruction of churches, and heavy financial penalties resulted in the steady decline in the number of Christians in Egypt. During the rule of the Circassian Mamluks (1382–1517) and the Ottoman Turks (1517–1805), the Coptic community slipped into a late-medieval dark age. The number of Copts is thought to have diminished to a mere 150,000, out of a total population of three million. Coptic monks inhabited only a handful of monasteries, of which one of the most important was Dayr al-Muharraq at al-Qusiya in Upper Egypt, a Holy Family site. Parish priests and monks were undoubtedly extremely pious, but their religion was restricted to the reiteration of the liturgies. The scholarship of the church fathers had disappeared.[92]

This same period saw a renewed interest in the sites associated with the Holy Family among European pilgrims. Between the thirteenth and fifteenth centuries, at least twenty-eight western travelers wrote descriptions of the crypt in the Church of Abu Sarga in Old Cairo, where the Holy Family is said to have found shelter.[93] The village of Matariya, northeast of Cairo, also enjoyed great popularity among Catholic pilgrims. Here, within a large balsam garden, was a pool where the Christ Child was believed to have bathed. In 1480, the Mamluk owner of the garden charged the Dominican friar Felix Fabri an entrance fee of six ducats. The price included permission to bathe in the pool. Felix Fabri also described an immense fig tree that had sheltered the Virgin. He made no mention of the sycamore, which is today venerated at Matariya as the Virgin's tree.[94]

Modern Egypt

In the eighteenth century, Egypt became a quasi-autonomous state within the Ottoman Empire. It was ruled by Mamluk beys, an oligarchy of Circassian military officers.[95] The beys paid an annual tribute to the sultan in Istanbul, but retained possession of most of Egypt's revenues. Copts were widely employed in the military households of the leading beys as financial administrators and scribes. Some of these Copts achieved great power and wealth. Ibrahim al-Jawhari (d. 1795) was the equivalent of a minister of finance during the joint reign of Ibrahim Bey and Murad Bey, the future opponents of Napoleon. He controlled the public income and expenditures of Egypt, as well as managed the personal fortune of Ibrahim Bey. The tax collectors and state scribes under his direction were almost exclusively Copts.[96] Ibrahim al-Jawhari was described by a Muslim contemporary as "surpassing all his countrymen in the attainment of glory, authority, and great fame. During his time, the churches and monasteries flourished, and he endowed on them many properties and lands. Besides, he arranged considerable amounts of money and grain to be sent regularly to them."[97] The Holy Family site in Ma'adi, the Church of the Virgin, was restored at this time by Girgis al-Jawhari (d. 1810), who succeeded his brother Ibrahim as head of the financial administration of the Mamluk beys.[98] During the brief French occupation of Egypt (1798–1801), Girgis was confirmed in his position by Napoleon. He was only dismissed from his post in 1805, after Muhammad 'Ali seized power.[99]

Under the patronage of Coptic notables, the conditions of the Copts began to improve. Their community's social and economic revival was reflected in a sudden resurgence of icon painting, and this artistic flowering included commemoration of the Holy Family's journey. The most famous painters of this period are Ibrahim al-Naskhi ('the scribe'), who was probably a Copt, and Yuhanna al-Armani al-Qudsi ('the Armenian from Jerusalem'). In the mid-eighteenth century, both artists and their assistants painted hundreds of icons that influenced a generation of Coptic painters.[100] An icon of the Flight by Ibrahim al-Naskhi, or his school, in the Church of the Virgin at Dayr al-Muharraq, departs from traditional iconography. Instead of showing the arrival of the Holy Family in Egypt, the artist depicts their departure.[101] An angel in the upper left corner brings news of Herod's death, as the Holy Family set off for Nazareth. After three and a half years in Egypt, the Christ Child now leads his mother by the hand, while Joseph follows behind with a white donkey. The choice of subject matter leaves little doubt that the icon was painted for Dayr al-Muharraq, the site where an angel of the Lord is said to have appeared in a dream to Joseph and instructed him to return to Israel. The unique subject also underscores the connection between sacred topography and imagery.

Muhammad 'Ali Pasha (1805–48) was an Ottoman soldier of fortune who rose to power in the years following the French evacuation of Egypt. In 1811, he consolidated his position by massacring the Mamluk beys in the citadel of Cairo. Muhammad 'Ali then introduced sweeping reforms aimed at modernizing Egypt as quickly as possible. One of his most enduring legacies was the introduction of the first secular system of education in the Middle East. Khedive Isma'il (1863–79), the grandson of Muhammad 'Ali, was an equally determined advocate of Westernization. He abolished slavery, established hundreds of schools, built the Suez Canal, and developed modern Cairo. Under Isma'il, European dress became the norm for government officials and members of the upper classes.[102]

At the same time, the Coptic Church was experiencing its own reform movement. Kyrillus (Cyril) IV (1854–61) assumed the patriarchal office with a comprehensive program to raise the educational standards of the Copts, especially the clergy. He founded modern schools, including the first school for girls in Egypt. The patriarch paid special attention to the teaching of Arabic, Coptic, and foreign languages. A printing press, the second one in Egypt, was imported from Europe in order to produce textbooks at a reasonable price. Kyrillus IV is known as the father of Coptic reform, but not all of his policies were popular. One of the patriarch's more controversial acts was the public burning of icons, which he believed were receiving excessive veneration.[103]

Despite the iconoclasm of Kyrillus IV, the

An icon by Ibrahim al-Naskhi (circa 1760) of the Holy Family departing Egypt for Nazareth, Church of the Virgin, Dayr al-Muharraq (drawing: Lyster)

production of icons flourished in nineteenth-century Egypt. The most prolific artist of the period was Anastasi al-Rumi al-Qudsi ('the Greek from Jerusalem'). Like Ibrahim al-Naskhi and Yuhanna al-Armani a hundred years before, he inspired a school of icon painters, which remained active until the 1870s.[104] A number of icons by Anastasi or his followers depict the flight into Egypt. Most of them follow the traditional iconographic image, which shows the Virgin and Christ Child riding a white horse or donkey, while Joseph follows. The trio is sometimes in the company of their maidservant, Salome. The Holy Family is depicted traveling in the country, but a walled city can usually be seen in the distance. It almost certainly represents the fortress of Babylon, which had a long association with the Holy Family, as well as being the most famous Coptic quarter in Cairo. This identification is particularly appropriate in two nineteenth-century icons, one by Anastasi, the other by a contemporary of his, from the Church of Abu Sarga, which is located within the fortress of Babylon. [105]

A variation on the traditional theme of the Flight, is found in an icon by Anastasi, dated 1833, in the Church of the Virgin at Ma'adi. It consists of ten scenes from the life of Mary.[106] The painting of the Flight shows the Virgin riding alone and Joseph carrying the Christ Child on his shoulders.[107] This image seems to derive from a literary source preserved in the Ethiopian *Narrative of the Virgin Mary*, which describes just such a scene.[108]

The era of social, economic, and cultural reform inaugurated by Muhammad 'Ali Pasha also saw the legal emancipation of the Copts. Sa'id Pasha (1854–63) abolished the poll tax imposed on Christians and Jews at the time of the Arab conquest. In 1879, Khedive Tawfiq (1879–92) proclaimed the equality of all Egyptians irrespective of their ethnic origin or religion. This was later formalized in a decree of 1913 and again in the Constitution of 1922.[109] The

new atmosphere of national communion and of shared citizenship resulted in the resistance to the British occupation (1882–1956) by Copts and Muslims alike. The symbol of the nationalist Wafd party, founded in 1919, was the combination of the crescent and the cross. The party's slogan was "Religion for God, and the motherland for all."[110]

After the 1952 revolution, the Coptic Church experienced an ecclesiastical renaissance. Patriarch Kyrillus VI (1959–71) laid the foundation for this great revival by inspiring the rejuvenation of monasticism. He groomed a new generation of church leaders drawn from university-educated monks. At the same time, the patriarch put an end to educational deficiencies among the clergy with his decree that all parish priests must be graduates of the Coptic Clerical College. Kyrillus VI also encouraged church building throughout Egypt. He obtained per-

An icon by Anastasi al-Rumi (1833) showing Joseph carrying the Christ Child, Church of the Virgin, Ma'adi (drawing: Lyster).

ⲀⲄⲄⲈⲖⲞⲤ · Ⲑ︤Ⲉ︥ⲞⲨ · ⲦⲐⲈⲞⲦⲞⲔⲞⲤ · ⲠⲒ ⲬⲒⲚⲦ︤Ⲁ︥Ⲥ︤Ⲑ︥Ⲟ ⲈⲂⲞⲖ ϧⲈⲚ ⲬⲎⲘⲒ · ⲒⲰⲤⲎⲪ ⲠⲒⲀⲘϢⲈ · ⲠⲬⲤ · ⲀⲄⲄⲈⲖⲞⲤ ⲔⲨⲢⲒⲞⲨ

A modern Egyptian icon of the Holy Family traveling on the Nile, by Yusif Girgis Ayad.

mission from President Gamal Abd al-Nasser to build a new cathedral in Cairo with an adjoining patriarchal residence. In 1968, the Cathedral of Saint Mark was consecrated in the presence of Nasser and Haile Selassie of Ethiopia. The new cathedral complex accommodates several centers of Coptic studies, and has become the urban, spiritual, and cultural nucleus of modern Coptic life.[111]

Under Shenuda III, the 117th successor of Saint Mark and the current patriarch, the Coptic Church has enjoyed a remarkable era of expansion. Coptic monasteries now contain more monks than at any time since the heroic era of the original desert fathers in the fourth and fifth centuries. There has also been an enormous increase in Coptic pilgrims, who visit monasteries and holy sites by the busload on weekends and feast days. One of the most impressive modern pilgrimage centers is the Convent of the Virgin at Durunka, south of Asyut. The monastic complex, which houses both monks and nuns, is built up the slope of a steep cliff. Its spiritual heart is a large cave where the Holy Family is believed to have stayed. The cave is one of the most unusual churches in Egypt. It is a large hall, measuring about twelve meters square, carved into the rock of the cliff. The mouth of the cliff faces east, the direction of prayer in Coptic churches. The altar is placed in a small, freestanding grilled enclosure in the center of the hall. No other architectural elements define the interior. This simple design allows for great flexibility of function in the church, and is ideal for accommodating large numbers of pilgrims.

The modern Coptic renaissance has inspired a flourishing school of icon painting. In 1956, Isaac Fanous was appointed director of the art and archaeology section of the patriarchate's Institute of Coptic Studies. He helped define a set of iconographic rules of painting, which have received the blessing of the Coptic Church. Fanous based his style on the ancient Coptic artistic tradition, and he works in mosaics, murals, and panel paintings. His sacred images can be found in Coptic churches all over the world, for example, the Cathedral of Saint Mark in Alexandria and the Church of the Virgin in Los Angeles. Most icon painters currently active in Egypt have trained under Fanous or his assistants at the Institute of Coptic Studies. Sacred images in his style are also mass produced as inexpensive posters, key chains, and bookmarks.[112]

The flight of the Holy Family is a popular subject in modern Coptic religious art. In recent years, variations of the traditional theme have appeared, most notably a depiction of the Holy Family in a boat on the Nile, set against the pyramids. This new image seems to be linked to the Church of the Virgin at Ma'adi, where the Holy Family are believed to have set sail for Upper Egypt. In the nineteenth century, the fortress of Babylon was used to represent Egypt in depictions of the Flight, while a hundred years later, the Nile and the pyramids indicate the setting. The change is significant. Babylon is predominantly a Christian site, but the pyramids and the Nile symbolize all of Egypt. Pope Shenuda III is adamant that the Copts are not a minority group in Egypt.[113] Instead, they are an essential part of a modern Egyptian society that includes both Christians and Muslims. Since the days of the nationalist movement, the pyramids have symbolized the unity of Egyptians. In modern Coptic icons of the Flight, the presence of the pyramids and the Nile indicate that the blessing of the Lord of hosts, promised by Isaiah and fulfilled by the Holy Family's journey through Egypt, is a gift for all of the country's inhabitants.

Notes

1   Bernhard W. Anderson, *The Living World of the Old Testament* (Harlow, U.K.: Longman, 1990), 306–7.
2   J. C. Fenton, *Saint Matthew* (London: Penguin Books, 1987), 17–19.
3   See Stephen J. Davis, chapter 3 of this book.
4   Ragheb Moftah, comp., *Coptic Orthodox Liturgy of St. Basil with Complete Musical Transcription* (Cairo: The American University in Cairo Press, 1999), 22.
5   Gerard Viaud, "Pilgrimage," *The Coptic Encyclopedia*, ed. Aziz S. Atiya (New York: Macmillan, 1991), 1969–71.
6   For modern accounts of the Holy Family's journey, see William F. Bassili, *The Flight into Egypt* (Cairo: Dar Memphis Press, 1968). Samir W. Farid, *The Flight into Egypt* (Cairo: Youssef Abdalla, 1965). Fathy S. Georgy, *The Holy Family in Egypt* (Cairo: Dar Nubar, 1998). Michael M. Iskander, *Jesus Christ in Egypt. The Events, Traditions and Sites of Halts during the Journey of the Holy Family into Egypt* (Cairo: Mahaba Bookshop, 1999). Otto F. A. Meinardus, *The Holy Family in Egypt* (Cairo: The American University in Cairo Press, 1986).

7   The Holy Synod sub-committee presided [over] by H.H. Pope Shenouda III,
     The Holy Family in Egypt (Marriout, Egypt: St. Mina Monastery, 2000).

8   Georgy, *Holy Family in Egypt*, 2; Meinardus, *Holy Family*, 25–26.

9   Farid, *Flight*, 31–32; Georgy, *Holy Family in Egypt*, 2–3; Meinardus, *Holy Family*, 31.

10   Iskandar, *Jesus Christ in Egypt*, 40–43; Meinardus, *Holy Family*, 31–32.

11   Farid, *Flight*, 35; Iskandar, *Jesus Christ in Egypt*, 54–55; Meinardus, *Holy Family*, 33.

12   Bassili, *Flight into Egypt*, 72; Georgy, *Holy Family in Egypt*, 4.

13   Iskandar, *Jesus Christ in Egypt*, 56–57; Meinardus, *Holy Family*, 34–35.

14   Farid, *Flight*, 56; Meinardus, *Holy Family*, 64.

15   Iskandar, *Jesus Christ in Egypt*, 57–60; Meinardus, *Holy Family*, 38–40.

16   Farid, *Flight*, 42; Meinardus, *Holy Family*, 40.

17   Iskandar, *Jesus Christ in Egypt*, 74; Meinardus, *Holy Family*, 63–64.

18   Bassili, *Flight into Egypt*, 78–79; Iskandar, *Jesus Christ in Egypt*, 61–62; Farid, *Flight*, 43–44.

19   Georgy, *Holy Family in Egypt*, 16–17; Meinardus, *Holy Family*, 47–48.

20   Meinardus, *Holy Family*, 48.

21   Farid, *Flight*, 51–52; Meinardus, *Holy Family*, 49–51.

22   See Davis, chapter 3.

23   Farid, *Flight*, 52–53; Meinardus, *Holy Family*, 52–53.

24   Bassili, *Flight into Egypt*, 88–91; Meinardus, *Holy Family*, 57–58.

25   Iskandar, *Jesus Christ in Egypt*, 71; Meinardus, *Holy Family*, 58–59.

26   B. T. A. Evetts, trans., and Alfred J. Butler, ed., *The Churches and Monasteries of Egypt
     and Some Neighbouring Countries, Attributed to Abu Salih the Armenian* (Oxford:
     Clarendon Press, 1969), 68.

27   D. S. Russell, *The Jews from Alexander to Herod* (Oxford: Oxford University Press,
     1967), 18–20.

28   Alan Unterman, *Dictionary of Jewish Lore and Legend* (London: Thames and Hudson,
     1991), 156.

29   W. H. C. Frend, *Martyrdom and Persecution in the Early Church* (Grand Rapids, MI:
     Baker Book House, 1991), 351.

30   W. H. C. Frend, *The Early Church. From the Beginnings to 461* (London: SCM Press,
     1991), 90.

31   Frend, *Martyrdom*, 452.

32   Eusebius, *The History of the Church*, trans. G. A. Williamson (Harmondsworth:
     Penguin Books, 1965), 337.

33   Frend, *Martyrdom*, 537.

34   Iskandar, *Jesus Christ in Egypt*, 55–56; Meinardus, *Holy Family*, 33–34.

35   Aziz S. Atiya, "Dimiyanah and Her Forty Virgins," *Coptic Encyclopedia*, 903.

36   Henry R. Percival, trans., *The Seven Ecumenical Councils of the Undivided Church*,
     vol. 14 of *Nicene and Post-Nicene Fathers of the Christian Church*, eds. Philip Schaff
     and Henry Wace (Edinburgh: T&T Clark, 1991), 3.

37   Gregory of Nazianze, quoted in Frend, *Early Church*, 153.

38   Richard Krautheimer, *Early Christian and Byzantine Architecture* (Harmondsworth:
     Penguin Books, 1981), 62.

39   The oldest dated churches in Egypt are fourth-century basilicas discovered at
     Kellis in the Dakhla oasis, see James E. Knudstad and Rosa A. Frey, "Kellis: The
     Architectural Survey of the Romano Byzantine Town at Ismant el-Kharab" in
     Reports from the Survey of the Dakhleh Oasis Western Desert of Egypt, eds., C.S.
     Churcher and A.J. Mills (Oxford; Oxbow Books, 1999), 189–214.

40   Peter Grossmann, "Architectural Elements of Churches: Khurus," *Coptic
     Encyclopedia*, 212–13.

41   H. Ellershaw, trans., "Life of Antony" in *St. Athanasius: Select Works and Letters*, vol. 4
     of *Nicene and Post-Nicene Fathers of the Christian Church*, eds. Philip Schaff and
     Henry Wace (Edinburgh: T&T Clark, 1991), 200.

42 Ellershaw, "Life of Antony," 208.

43 Robert T. Meyer, trans., *Palladius: The Lausiac History* (New York: Newman, 1964), 40.

44 For more information on the desert fathers, see Benedicta Ward, trans., *The Sayings of the Desert Fathers. The Alphabetical Collection* (Kalamazoo, MI: Cistercian Publications, 1984).

45 René-George Coquin and Peter Grossmann, "Dayr Abu Hinnis," *Coptic Encyclopedia*, 701-3.

46 Nicole Thierry, "Les peintures de Deir Abou Hennis," *Solidarite-Orient*, 207 (1998): 5-16.

47 In contrast to most later depictions, the iconography of the Flight used in the mosaics at S. Maria Maggiore (432-40) in Rome is very different. There, the Holy Family is shown on foot, accompanied by angels, being welcomed into the town of Sotina, after the miracle of the falling idols. Gertrud Schiller, *Iconography of Christian Art*, vol. 1 (Greenwich, CT: New York Graphic Society, 1971), 118 and figs. 309-10.

48 Schiller, *Iconography*, 119. Thierry also remarks on the iconographic influence of the Journey to Bethlehem on depictions of the Flight. Thierry, "Deir Abou Hennis," 10.

49 Painted apse from the Monastery of Apa Apollo at Bawit of Christ Pantocrator and enthroned Virgin and Child, Coptic Museum, Cairo (inv. 7118), illustrated in Gawdat Gabra, *Cairo: The Coptic Museum & Old Churches* (Cairo: Egyptian International Publishing—Longman, 1993), 58–59.

50 Painted apse from Apa Jeremias at Saqqara of Christ Pantocrator and enthroned Theotokos, Coptic Museum, Cairo (inv. 7987), illustrated in Nabil Selim Atalla, *Coptic Art, Volume I, Wall-Paintings* (Cairo: Lehnert, and Landrock, n.d.), 21.

51 Gustav Kühnel, *Wall Paintings in the Latin Kingdom of Jerusalem* (Berlin: Gebr. Mann Verlag, 1988), 190.

52 Moftah, *Coptic Orthodox Liturgy*, 23.

53 Painted apse from Apa Jeremias at Saqqara of the Galaktotrophousa, Coptic Museum, Cairo (inv. 8002), illustrated in J.E. Quibell, *Excavations at Saqqara (1908–9, 1909–10). The Monastery of Apa Jeremias* (Cairo: Institut Français d'Archéologie Orientale du Caire, 1912), plate 22.

54 For a thorough introduction to this challenging subject, see the first chapter of W. H. C. Frend, *The Rise of the Monophysite Movement* (Cambridge: Cambridge University Press, 1979).

55 Aziz S. Atiya, *A History of Eastern Christianity* (London: Methuen, 1968), 69.

56 Frend, *Early Church*, 233.

57 Frend, *Monophysite Movement*, 273–76.

58 Frend, *Monophysite Movement*, 285.

59 B. T. A. Evetts, trans., *History of the Patriarchs of the Egyptian Church* (Paris: Patrologia Orientalist, 1904), 72.

60 Bernard Lewis, *Islam from the Prophet Muhammad to the Capture of Constantinople, Volume II: Religion and Society* (Oxford: Oxford University Press, 1974), 217–19.

61 Stanley Lane-Poole, *A History of Egypt in the Middle Ages* (London: Methuen, 1901), 32.

62 Sam I. Gellens, "Islamization of Egypt," *Coptic Encyclopedia*, 938.

63 André Ferré, "Fatimids and the Copts," *Coptic Encyclopedia*, 1097–8.

64 Mark R. Cohen, *Jewish Self-Government in Medieval Egypt* (Princeton: Princeton University Press, 1980), 69.

65 Aziz S. Atiya, Yassa 'Abd al-Masih, and O. H. E. Khs-Burmester, eds. and trans., *History of the Patriarchs of the Egyptian Church*, Vol. 2:2 (Cairo: Société d'Archeologie Copte, 1948), 138.

66 Aziz S. Atiya, "Sawirus ibn al-Muqaffa'," *Coptic Encyclopedia*, 2101.

67 Terry G. Wilfong, "The non-Muslim communities: Christian communities" in *The Cambridge History of Egypt, Volume One, Islamic Egypt, 640–1517* ed., Carl F. Petry (Cambridge: Cambridge University Press, 1998), 184–86.

68 Atiya, 'Abd al-Masih, and Khs-Burmester, *History of the Patriarchs*, 140–46. Abu al-Makarim/Abu Salih tells the same story, but places it in the reign of Caliph al-'Aziz (975–96) during the patriarchate of Anba Ephraim. In both accounts, permission to rebuild the Church of Saint Mercurius was granted after the patriarch performed the miracle of moving one of the peaks of the Muqattam hills, east of Cairo. For more information, see Evetts, *Churches and Monasteries*, 116–19.

69 Yaacov Lev, *State and Society in Fatimid Egypt* (Leiden: E.J. Brill, 1991), 29.

70 Lev, *Fatimid Egypt*, 60.

71 For information on the life of Salah al-Din, see Malcolm Cameron Lyons and D. E. P. Jackson, *Saladin. The Politics of Holy War* (Cambridge: Cambridge University Press, 1982).

72 For more on the Ayyubid dynasty, see R. Stephen Humphreys, *From Saladin to the Mongols. The Ayyubids of Damascus, 1193–1260* (Albany, NY: State University of New York, 1977).

73 Antoine Khater and O. H. E. Khs-Burmester, trans., *History of the Patriarchs of the Egyptian Church*, Vol. 4:1 (Cairo: Société d'Archeologie Copte, 1974), 98.

74 For details on church revenues under the Fatimids, see Evetts, *Churches and Monasteries*, 15.

75 Evetts, *Churches and Monasteries*, 347–52.

76 Wooden altar from the Church of Abu Sarga (ca. fifth century), Coptic Museum, Cairo (inv. 1172), illustrated in Gabra, *Coptic Museum*, 93.

77 Gabra, *Coptic Museum*, 118–21. O. H. E. Khs-Burmester, *A Guide to the Ancient Coptic Churches of Cairo* (Cairo: Société d'Archeologie Copte, 1955), 18–23. Otto F. A. Meinardus, *The Historic Coptic Churches of Cairo* (Cairo: Philopatron-Translation and Publishing House, 1994), 20–25.

78 O. H. E. Khs-Burmester, *A Guide to the Monasteries of the Wadi 'n-Natrun* (Cairo: Société d'Archeologie Copte, 1955), 13–14.

79 Karel Innemée, Luk Van Rompay, and Elizabeth Sobczynski, "Deir Al-Surian (Egypt): Its Wall-paintings, Wall-texts and Manuscripts." *Hugoye, Journal of Syriac Studies* 2:2 (1999), http://syrcom.cua.edu/Hugoye/.

80 Peter Grossmann, "Neue Beobachtungen zur al-Adra Kirche von Dair as-Suryan," *Nubian Letters* 19 (1993): 1–8.

81 Isa. 7:14, Exod. 3:2, Ezek. 44:2, and Dan. 2:34.

82 Paul Van Moorsel, "Deir as Sourian Revisited," *Nubian Letters* 17 (1992): 1–13.

83 Lucy-Anne Hunt, "The Fine Incense of Virginity: a late twelfth century wallpainting of the Annunciation at the Monastery of the Syrians, Egypt," *Byzantine and Modern Greek Studies* 19 (1995): 182–233.

84 The paintings of this third phase are illustrated in Jules Leroy, *Les Peintures des Couvents du Ouadi Natroun* (Cairo: Institute Français d'Archéologie Orientale du Caire, 1982). The Annunciation-Nativity is in plates 107–24, the Ascension in plates 125–35, and the Dormition in plates 136–46.

85 Karel C. Innemée, et al., "New Discoveries in the Al-'Adra' Church of Dayr As-Suryan in the Wadi Al-Natrun," *Mitteilungen zur Christlichen Archäologie* 4 (1998): 86–87. The Galaktotrophousa is dated here to the second half of the seventh century.

86 Lucy-Anne Hunt, "Christian-Muslim Relations in Painting in Egypt of the Twelfth to mid-Thirteenth Centuries," *Cahiers Archéologiques* 33 (1985), 111–54.

87 Coptic Gospels, Cairo, 1249–50, Institut Catholique Copte-Arabe 1, Paris, illustrated in Jules Leroy, *Les Manuscrits Coptes et Coptes-Arabes Illustrés*

(Paris: Librairie Orientaliste Paul Geuthner, 1974), color plates E–G and plates 75–92. The Pauline and Catholic Epistles and Acts from the same manuscript are in the Coptic Museum, Cairo (Bibl. 94), see Leroy, *Manuscrits Coptes*, plates 93–95.

88 Institut Catholique Copte-Arabe 1, folio 4v, illustrated in Leroy, *Manuscrits coptes*, plate 77.

89 Lewis, *Islam*, 229, 231–32. For a survey of the Bahri Mamluk sultanate, see Robert Irwin, *The Middle East in the Middle Ages: The Early Mamluk Sultanate, 1250–1382* (Beckenham, Kent, U.K.: Croom Helm, 1986).

90 Donald P. Little, "Coptic Conversion to Islam under the Bahri Mamluks," *Bulletin of the School of Oriental and African Studies*, 39 (1976): 567–68.

91 Al-Maqrizi, quoted in Little, "Coptic Conversion," 568.

92 Aziz S. Atiya, "Copts under the Ottomans," *Coptic Encyclopedia*, 1857.

93 Maurice Martin, "Pilgrims and Travelers in Christian Egypt," *Coptic Encyclopedia*, 1977.

94 Meinardus, *Holy Family*, 38–40.

95 For information on the eighteenth-century Mamluk Beylicate, see Jane Hathaway, *The Politics of Households in Ottoman Egypt* (Cambridge: Cambridge University Press, 1997).

96 Harald Motzki, "Ibrahim al-Jawhari," *Coptic Encyclopedia*, 1274.

97 Abd al-Rahman al-Jabarti, quoted in Tadros Yacoub Malaty, *Introduction to the Coptic Orthodox Church* (Alexandria: St. George's Coptic Orthodox Church, 1993), 161.

98 Meinardus, *Historic Coptic Churches*, 82.

99 Harald Motzki, "Jirgis al-Jawhari," *Coptic Encyclopedia*, 1332–34.

100 Mat Immerzeel, "Coptic Art," in *Between Desert and City: The Coptic Orthodox Church Today*, eds. Nelly van Doorn-Harder and Karin Vogt (Oslo: Novus Forlag, 1997), 278–79.

101 Illustrated in Nabil Selim Atalla, *The Escape to Egypt According to Coptic Tradition* (Cairo: Lehnert and Landrock, 1993), 60.

102 For more on the Muhammad 'Ali Dynasty prior to the British occupation, see F. Robert Hunter, *Egypt Under the Khedives 1805–1879* (Cairo: The American University in Cairo Press, 1999; Pittsburgh: University of Pittsburgh Press, 1984).

103 Mounir Shoucri, "Cyril IV," *Coptic Encyclopedia*, 677–79.

104 Immerzeel, "Coptic Art," 279.

105 The Abu Sarga icons are illustrated in Atalla, *Escape to Egypt*, cover photograph, 31.

106 Illustrated in Nabil Selim Atalla, *Coptic Icons*, vol. 1 (Cairo: Lehnert and Landrock, 1998), 15; *Escape to Egypt*, 44.

107 The Coptic Museum in Cairo has an icon (inv. 3350) assigned to the eighteenth century with the same subject matter. See Gabra, *Coptic Museum*, 82.

108 See Davis, chapter 3.

109 Aziz S. Atiya, "Kibt," *The Encyclopaedia of Islam* (Leiden, 1960–), 5:94.

110 Christian van Nispen tot Sevenaer, "Changes in Relations between Copts and Muslims (1952–1994)," in van Doorn-Harder and Vogt, *Between Desert and City*, 25.

111 Nelly van Doorn-Harder, "Kyrillos VI (1902–1971): Planner, Patriarch and Saint," in van Doorn-Harder and Vogt, *Between Desert and City*, 236–38.

112 Immerzeel, "Coptic Art," 279–80. Stéphane René, Ch. Chaillot, and Monica René, "Isaac Fanous," *Le Monde Copte* 18 (1990): 5–13.

113 John Watson, "Signposts to Biography—Pope Shenouda III" in van Doorn-Harder and Vogt, *Between Desert and City*, 248.

Tracing the Route of the Holy Family Today

Cornelis Hulsman

The tradition of the journey of the Holy Family into Egypt, through the Nile Delta, up the Nile Valley, and back again to Palestine is fascinating because it is a living ancient tradition that shows how strongly Egyptian Christians throughout the ages have wanted to be connected to Jesus and the Bible, which mentions Egypt more often than any country other than Israel. Those who found refuge in Egypt include Abraham and his wife Sarah; Joseph, his brothers, and his father Jacob; Moses; and the Holy Family.

For this chapter all sites associated with the sojourn of the Holy Family in Egypt were visited, and local bishops, priests, and believers were interviewed. The interviews reveal a story that is in continuous development. Some sites have been forgotten, recent discoveries have been made, and local traditions have added locations to the route. Some of them have received a place on the official itinerary, while others have only local importance. Regardless, the tradition is very much alive.

The Holy Family and the Bible

Coptic Orthodox priests and bishops consistently refer to the Bible when asked about the Holy Family. That is obviously the basis of their belief in the story of the Holy Family, which serves as a link between the Bible and the contemporary church in Egypt. What are these biblical references?

For Father Philoxenos of the Monastery of al-Muharraq, the history of the Coptic Orthodox Church and the flight of the Holy Family into Egypt starts with Isaiah 19:19, which prophesies an altar in the midst of Egypt. "The church in Egypt is the only church in the world that has been prophesied in the Old Testament," he says. Isaiah 19:1 speaks about the Lord riding on a swift cloud to Egypt. "Who else is this but our Lord Jesus?" says Father Philoxenos, who interprets the cloud as a way to describe the Holy Virgin.

A Priest points to the footprint of baby Jesus on the stone that was discovered by workers just outside the Church of the Holy Virgin at Sakha.

The prophecy of Isaiah is a clear attack on the religion of the ancient pharaohs, and Metropolitan Athanasius of Beni Suef explains it as "a prophecy of the struggles between Christians and non-Christians in the first centuries when Christianity began to grow, but the established religious and ruling class tried to stop it. It wasn't an easy struggle, and many believers paid with their lives. The prophecy says the believers in God will cry out to the Lord because of their oppressors, and the Egyptians will come to acknowledge the Lord. This happened," says Metropolitan Athanasius, "in the centuries prior to the Arab conquest of Egypt. Egyptians, therefore became, as Isaiah 19:25 says, a blessed people."

The prophecies against the old pharaonic religion mention several prominent cities by name; Memphis is mentioned in Isaiah 19:13. Jeremiah (43:13) prophesied that the sacred pillars of On and the temples of the gods of Egypt would be destroyed.

Ezekiel prophesied, in chapters 29 and 30, that Egypt's pharaoh, described as the "great monster," would be punished. Egypt's young men would fall by the sword, the yoke of pharaonic Egypt would be broken, and her proud strength would come to an end. Bubastis is explicitly mentioned in this chapter (30:17).

The Egyptologist and professional tour guide Lutfi Sharif points to the fact that Egypt's early Christians deliberately founded large churches in the centers of paganism, and certainly in the cities mentioned in the above prophecies. It was foretold that these centers would crumble, and, as Metropolitan Athanasius explains, "thus these early Christians knew they would overcome the hardship of being in these pagan centers."

Egyptian Christians also refer to Hosea 11:1: "Out of Egypt I have called my son." The Holy Family found refuge in Egypt but also returned to Palestine, where Jesus' mission for the salvation of the world had to be fulfilled.

Matthew 2:13–23 mentions the flight into Egypt, where the family stayed until an angel told Joseph to take the family and return to Nazareth. Most Western Christians would refer first to these passages, but not so in Egypt. Father Philoxenos makes it abundantly clear that for the Egyptian Church, the flight into Egypt starts with the prophecy in Isaiah.

In addition to the above-mentioned Biblical references, Egyptians also make comparisons with Jesus' ministry in Palestine, where he performed many miracles. According to tradition, he did likewise in Egypt. He was the living water, but did not forget the physical needs of the people; thus, during his ministry in Egypt, he created many wells, giving the purest water of all.

The church in Egypt strongly believes that the visit of the Holy Family to Egypt prepared the hearts of the Egyptians to receive Jesus' message of salvation. By A.D. 60, Saint Mark had already arrived. The spread of Christianity in Egypt was fast, but not without struggles. Just as Jesus was often rejected in many cities in Egypt, so did early Christians feel the rejection of their pagan neighbors, but they were confident in the knowledge that it was prophesied that their faith in Jesus would triumph.

Thus the story of the Holy Family became the link between the Bible and the church in Egypt, a unique link that no other church in the world can claim.

Pilgrimage

The locations the Holy Family visited have become holy places, where *nahda*s are organized to commemorate the death or martyrdom of a saint. A *nahda* is a period of three to fifteen days prior to day the saint is remembered, in which the church organizes daily prayers and invites well-known spiritual people, both clergy and non-clergy, to speak about spiritual subjects. Organizing a *nahda* is the responsibility of an individual church and is often related to the patron saint of that church. Only the *nahda* of the

Holy Virgin in August seems to be celebrated nationwide. At several locations the commemoration of the arrival of the Holy Family in Egypt has been turned into a *nahda*. Father Serabamun of the Church of Saint Barbara in Old Cairo explained that some *nahda*s attracted so many people that they turned into a *mulid*, or pilgrimage festival. The word *mulid* comes from the Arabic word for birthday, but generally *mulid*s celebrate the date of death or martyrdom of a saint, because Christians believe that this was the day the saint was reborn in everlasting life.

"*Nahda*s and *mulid*s are generally organized at the same time, but the difference between a *nahda* and a *mulid* is that a *nahda* is spiritual while *mulid*s have become a folk tradition where people primarily come for enjoyment," Father Serabamun explains. "*Nahda*s are organized, just as prayer meetings, within the church building, but when the number of people becomes too large and expands inside the church compound and outside its premises, the church often cannot control it any more and people start organizing non-spiritual activities such as making music and selling their products." *Mulid*s today can attract anywhere from a thousand to hundreds of thousands of pilgrims. At only a few sites, where no Christian community is left, has the tradition of organizing *nahda*s and *mulid*s died out.

At the holy sites, whether during *nahda*s and *mulid*s or outside the yearly festivals, large flocks of people have come for centuries to pray and ask for miraculous healings. Women come to pray for a child or anything that is important in their personal life.

Pilgrimage centers need to have something that pilgrims can see and touch. This ranges from relics, icons, and objects a saint used, to natural objects such as a well, a cave, or a tree. The acutely sensory experience is important for many believers. It makes their faith more tangible, and brings the mysterious within their reach.

Christians flock in large numbers to the shrines hoping for blessing, or *baraka*, which could be anything from the prayer of a priest, feeling closeness to God near a picture of a saint, a little plastic cylinder full of oil, a miraculous healing, or participation in a Holy Eucharist. At most pilgrimage sites stories are told about miraculous healings, and some pilgrimage centers have published accounts of them in booklets. These stories themselves serve to attract new pilgrims.

Pilgrimage centers are generally more prosperous than other places of Christian worship. Pilgrims come to bring their gifts, especially after a prayer has been heard or a healing has taken place. Believers often make a *nadr*, or vow, to visit the pilgrimage center and make a gift or offering if they themselves, or a person dear to them, is healed or if a person is successful, for example, in an examination.

Most pilgrimage sites are also popular places where believers come with their newborn children for baptisms, because they believe that a baptism at a pilgrimage site will bring an extra blessing for the child.

All pilgrimage sites sell souvenirs, which can be small plastic statues of the Holy Virgin or a saint, or cups, pens, scarves, and other objects with the picture of a saint printed on them. Pilgrimage centers usually do a flourishing trade during a *mulid*, and local traders come to sell their wares, refreshments, and food. Several Christians visiting these events said they rarely entered the church, because it was too crowded, and explained that they came for amusement and social contact.

Christian *mulid*s attract Muslims as well. Some hope for a blessing or a miraculous healing, but many come just to enjoy the atmosphere and join their Christian friends in the festivities.

Many Orthodox bishops and priests do not recommend their faithful to visit the pilgrimage sites during *mulid*s. "Our Coptic Orthodox Church has developed a policy in the past twenty-five to thirty years to change *mulid*s into spiritual events," Father Serabamun says. He explains that when he became the priest of the church of Saint Barbara in Old Cairo in 1981 he found the yearly celebration had some of the elements of a *mulid,* such as music. "We stopped the elements that aimed at amusement and made it a *nahda,*" he says. Metropolitan Athanasius of Beni Suef and Bishop Arsanius of Minya encourage their faithful to visit the pilgrimage sites when it is quiet so that they might find time for prayer and reading from the Scripture. For both leaders, the hustle and bustle of the *mulid*s brings no spiritual benefit. "It is not seeing and touching at specific moments that is important, but the direct relationship between believer and creator," Bishop Arsanius explains.

But not all places seem to discourage the faithful from visiting the *mulid*s, which also bring income for a church. Some bishops and priests say they cannot forbid people to visit *mulid*s because they may have made *nadr*s, or vows, to visit a *mulid* or present gifts then. Yousef Sidhom, editor-in-chief of the Christian weekly *Watani,* understands the church's focus on the spiritual element but says, "I wouldn't like to lose this folk tradition because it brings Muslims and Christians together and strengthens our being Egyptian together."

The Sites Associated with the Holy Family

As in the days of old, there is debate about the itinerary the Holy Family followed. Certain places are generally accepted, while others are not commonly mentioned, and sometimes places are mentioned that are not on the official map of the church.

Some of the recent additions to the itinerary fall within accepted tradition. Other stories, however, are clearly in opposition to the tradition. Bishop Demetrius of Mallawi says that some claim the Holy Family went as far south as Dayr al-Ganadla near Abu Tig. Still others claim the Holy Family went to Akhmim, south of Suhag. According to Ethiopian traditions, the Holy Family even went south to Ethiopia. The Coptic Orthodox Church, however, does not accept sites that are clearly outside the route the church has accepted. But once a claim is made for a site that lies on the route, church leaders do not oppose it. "Perhaps it is true and perhaps it is not," several bishops remarked when asked about other sites in their dioceses that were not on the official route.

In this text we will follow the officially recognized route of the Coptic Orthodox Church, including not only the sites marked by the church, but also those that are mentioned by local parishioners, priests, and bishops along the way. The stories cited are the stories as they are told by local Christians.

Entering Egypt

The flight into Egypt began from Bethlehem. The Holy Family first went to Gaza and Rafah (Raphia), where no remains of ancient Christianity have been found. They then crossed Wadi al-'Arish, also called the River of Egypt, a small stream that has always formed the natural boundary between Egypt and Palestine. On Bashans 24 (June 1), the Holy Family entered Egypt.

The Holy Family continued to al-'Arish (in the Roman period called Rhinocolura) and al-Zaraniq (also called al-Filusiyat), where the remains of a castle and three old churches can be found. The flight went from al-Zaraniq to Tell al-Farama (or Farma), which in Roman and Byzantine times was known as Pelusium.

Farma or Pelusium, twenty kilometers east of modern Port Said and about five kilometers inland from the Mediterranean sea, was once a port and trading center, surrounded by marshes. Today one finds an elevation at the place where a castle once stood. Another elevation, a ridge

The remains of a church dating back to the fifth/sixth century at Tell al-Farma, North Sinai. Because a number of churches have been found on the high ground, the area has been called the Hill of the Churches.

about ten meters high and three kilometers long, is where archaeologists have found the remains of a number of ancient churches that date from between the fifth and seventh centuries. For that reason this ridge has become known as the Churches' Hill.

Tell Basta and Zaqaziq

The official itinerary of the Coptic Orthodox Church mentions Tell Basta, or Bubastis, two kilometers south of Zaqaziq, as the first city the Holy Family visited in the Delta. Today Tell Basta is no more then a field of stones and rocks with a large cat cemetery, but in the Twenty-second Dynasty (945–720 B.C.) it was a powerful political center and even Egypt's capital at one point. The names Tell Basta and Bubastis come from Pi-Beseth or Per-Bastet, which was the domain of Bastet, the cat goddess.

When the Holy Family was close to the once proud and prosperous city of Tell Basta, they encountered two brigands, Titus, an Egyptian,

and Dumachus, a Syrian. The Syrian wanted to rob them of their clothes because their garments were so luxurious. The Egyptian refused to attack them, but later they stole Jesus' silver sandals. When the Holy Virgin discovered this she wept, but Jesus comforted her and created a well,

An opening in a hill leading to some of the ruins at Tell al-Farma in North Sinai.

The ruins of ancient Egyptian temples at Tell Basta.

The well at Tell Basta that Jesus created, according to Coptic tradition.

The interior of the Church of the Holy Virgin and Saint John in Zaqaziq. The decor of the church, including the paintings on the doors before the altar, is in the Greek Orthodox fashion. The Coptic church chose to restore the church to its original Greek Orthodox style.

The interior of the Church of the Holy
Virgin and Saint John in Zaqaziq.
Originally a Greek Orthodox Church built
in 1925, it was bought by the Coptic
Orthodox church, which celebrated its first
liturgy here in July 1995. This is one of
three churches that is believed to stand in
the vicinity of where Klum's House stood.

saying: "Let this water help make whole and heal the souls and bodies of all those who shall drink of it, with the exception of the inhabitants of this town, of whom none shall be healed by it."[1]

There is, however, a second story explaining the creation of a well in Tell Basta. When the Holy Family approached the town, Jesus asked for food and water, and Mary walked to the town, but no one would give her food or water. Fortunately, a farmer called Klum was just then returning home from work in the fields, and saw they were strangers and had nothing to eat or drink. Mary explained that they were escaping from the soldiers of Herod. Klum invited them to his house, where Jesus healed Klum's paralyzed wife.

The next day Klum took them to see a religious festival in honor of Bastet, the cat goddess. According to tradition, as soon as Mary set foot inside the temple with the Christ Child in her arms, the granite statues fell and shattered, fulfilling the prophecy of Isaiah 19:1. Jesus not only scattered the idols, he also created a well in the temple, but the people of Tell Basta refused to give up their old faith and did not want to accept Jesus as Lord. Soldiers came and tried to arrest them, but Klum helped the Holy Family hide in the fields. The water became a source of healing for all but those who had rejected Jesus.

Before the Holy Family continued their flight, Jesus blessed Klum and his family and their home. "Jesus told his mother that any place they [the Holy Family] would visit and where people would welcome them, a church would be built in her name in which all people would come to pray and worship."[2] Bishop Yacobus of Zaqaziq believes that the Mar Girgis Church was built on the place where a fourth-century church once stood, which in turn had been built on the site of Klum's house.[3]

While Klum's house—and thus later the main churches of Zaqaziq—was blessed, the city of Bubastis has been severely punished for refusing to accept Jesus, priests say. Its young men fell by the sword, the yoke of pharaonic Egypt was bro-

ken, and its proud strength came to an end, as was prophesied by Ezekiel.

In 1991 Mahmud 'Umar,[4] professor of archaeologist at the University of Zaqaziq, discovered a well in the temple and pointed out that it could be dated to the first century. But the announcement that archaeologists had discovered the well Jesus created came only in 1997. "We didn't make the link to the Holy Family immediately—that took time," 'Umar explains. "We later found that medieval manuscripts, attributed to Pope Theophilus and Bishop Zacharias and a later work called *Kitab mayamir wa 'aja'ib al-'adhrâ'* ['Book of the Manuscripts and Miracles of the Holy Virgin'] mentioned that Jesus created a well in the temple. Only when we found that the description in the manuscripts matched our discovery did we make the news public that we had found the well Jesus created." Other Egyptian archaeologists, however, dispute Mahmud 'Umar's conclusions, arguing that more than this one well in the area can be dated to the same period.[5]

Musturud

The Holy Family, who were still being sought by Herod's soldiers, continued to Musturud, which today has become part of greater Cairo, on the agricultural road from Cairo to Bilbays and Ismailia.

After a long day of traveling, the Holy Family was in need of shelter and water. At Musturud they found a cave that gave them shelter and at that spot, just as he had in Tell Basta, Jesus created a well, which the Holy Family used for drinking, washing, and bathing. (The story of the creation of a well is a recurring one, and to the Copts this is important, as it demonstrates that Jesus, as Creator, whom all nature obeys, was already showing signs of this as a child.)

The use of the cave and the creation of the well made the place holy, and it was called al-Mahamma ('bathing place') because Jesus bathed in the water that came from this well. Father Abd al-Masih Bassit, the priest of the Church of the Virgin Mary at Musturud, showed us the

The interior of the church of Mar Girgis at Bilbays. In the corner stands a small model of the old church, which was built in the nineteenth century and replaced in the 1960s.

well, now located inside the church. Believers drink from it in the belief that this will bring them healing and *baraka*.

The other major site inside the church is a small cave where people come for individual prayers. The walls of the cave are gray from the many devout hands that have touched them. Father Bassit likes to tell the faithful that in ancient days the crypt was situated below a pharaonic temple dating to the days of Ramses II, who is believed to have been the pharaoh in the days of Moses. Because of its age, the cave has even more importance for pilgrims.

Bilbays

From Musturud the Holy Family turned north again and went to Bilbays, forty-eight kilometers northeast of Cairo. Father Mina of the Mar Girgis church in Bilbays explains that the tradition of the Holy Family's visit here was described by the seventh-century Bishop Zacharias of Sakha.[6] At the moment the Holy Family entered the town, a funeral procession was just leaving. Jesus felt compassion for the mourners and raised the dead man, the son of a widow, to life. The raised man then declared, "This is the True God, the savior of the world, who is born of the Blessed Virgin, who accomplished a mystery which the human intellect cannot comprehend," and all the inhabitants of Bilbays believed in Jesus.[7]

A young boy chases geese on a roof alongside the Church of Mar Girgis in the center of Bilbays. This new church was built in the 1960s.

Christians in Bilbays remember their city once had a tree dedicated to the Holy Virgin. Some say Napoleon's soldiers cut it down to use as firewood. Others say the tree fell when the nearby mosque of 'Umar al-'Ansari or houses in the town were extended.

Bilbays has only a small Coptic community today. The city has only one church, divided into upper and lower sections, which was built in 1932 and is surrounded by a huge wall. The lower section still has the nineteenth-century altar screen from the previous church. In the upper section is a model of the old church that probably dates back to the nineteenth century. The local Christian community believes that this church must have been built on the place of a much older one and that the first church may have been built in the fourth century.

Daqadus

From Bilbays the the Holy Family traveled via Zaqaziq to Daqadus, a village three kilometers north of the town of Mit Ghamr, north of Cairo and east of the eastern branch of the Nile. According to Bishop Philippus of Daqahliya, the name Daqadus comes from the Coptic *ti theotokos athokotos*, which means 'the mother of God of Daqadus.'

The only thing known to local believers is that Daqadus is a place where the Holy Family was well received. For that reason Daqadus became a blessed site throughout the ages.

The Church of the Holy Virgin at Daqadus looks onto the green fields on the outskirts of town.

A cross above the entrance to the church compound at Daqadus.

Following pages: Crosses on the domes above the church at Daqadus.

The well in the compound of the Church of the Holy Virgin at Daqadus, that is said to have been blessed by the Holy Family.

Bishop Philippus explains why the church in Daqadus was dedicated to the Holy Virgin: "Jesus prophesied that in each place the Holy Family visited a church would be built in the name of the Holy Virgin. That also happened in Daqadus." Bishop Philippus says that the current church, which dates from 1888, stands on the same spot that an old church dating back to 1239 stood, but disappeared during a flood at the beginning of the nineteenth century. The bishop believes this medieval church stood on the spot of a fourth-century church that was founded by Empress Helena (ca. 250–330), mother of the first Christian emperor Constantine. Inside the modern church compound is an ancient well, which, believers say, was blessed by the Holy Family when they stopped in Daqadus.

Samannud

Herod's soldiers were still searching for the Christ Child, so the Holy Family fled Daqadus and went to Samannud, which was once an important city in pharaonic and Ptolemaic times.

Pilgrims touch the water inside a large granite bowl that the Virgin Mary is said to have baked bread in. The bowl sits in the church courtyard at Samannud and pilgrims come to this site to get blessings from a number of objects, including the bowl.

The priests of the Church of Apa Anub in Samannud say the Holy Family stayed between fourteen and seventeen days in the town, where they were warmly welcomed by the local population. The Virgin Mary asked the child Jesus to bless the city and its people, and Jesus responded, "In this city there will be a church blessed forever in my name and in your name."[8] Father Abanub, one of the priests of the church, explains that during the time the Holy Family was in Egypt, Jesus wanted to distinguish between a house of worship in his name and those in the name of pagan idols. "This distinction is not needed today because all churches are churches of God and thus Jesus' name does not need to be explicitly mentioned in the name of the church. Of course the name of Apa Anub was added later in the history of the church."

According to tradition Jesus gave special blessings to the well, and Mary baked her bread in a large granite bowl, which, for that reason, became an object of blessing. Both the well and the bowl can be seen today in the church's courtyard. The well is covered to prevent dirt from falling in. Water is pumped up via a purification installation and is given to people to drink.

Samannud was the scene of terrible massacres under the Roman emperor Diocletian (r. 284–305). Priests say that on one occasion, eight thousand people, mostly young children, were killed for refusing to bow down before the Roman idols. One of these children was the twelve-year-old Apa Anub, to whom this church is dedicated, along with the Virgin. The church's popularity is primarily thanks to this saint. Most pilgrims come on July 31, when the martyrdom of Apa Anub is commemorated, and bring their children in the hope they will be blessed or healed. Many miracles are linked to this church, which has produced three booklets that tell of miracles in recent years. One of them is about a boy in a wheelchair who repeatedly came to the church to pray and ask the intercession of Apa Anub. On one of his visits, he suddenly felt he could walk,

and he did, to the great surprise and joy of his family and friends. He walked on to the shrine of Apa Anub, albeit with difficulty, while people were cheering and encouraging him. People cried for joy and praised God for this miracle. The church keeps the wheelchair in one of the windows as evidence of the miracle that happened.

Some pilgrims travel hundreds of kilometers to pray or to show their gratitude to the saint. A woman named Mariam traveled nearly one thousand kilometers, from Kom Ombo, north of Aswan, to pray at the sanctuary of Apa Anub for her eight-year-old son who had epilepsy. "My doctor told me five years ago to give my son 'Atif a certain medicine, but also told me he didn't know whether it would work. So we came to this church and prayed during the Holy Week [the week before Easter], asking for the medicine to work. Not much later we went to the doctor, and he told us the medicine really had worked. Improvements could already be seen in just three months. The doctor told us this was a miracle, and we came back to Apa Anub to thank him. We now come every year to his church to pray. This is the fourth year we have come."

Father Yu'annis of the church in Samannud listened to the story and commented, "People come and ask for prayers. We pray for them, and God helps and works miracles if this is his will. Some people come back and explain what has happened. We only register the miracles that are doc-

umented by qualified medical doctors. If a doctor has seen the healing of a child that he cannot explain using medical reasons, we can accept the miracle. We cannot take just any story people tell us. We have to avoid calling psychological effects miracles. A psychological effect comes temporarily then disappears, but a miracle remains."

While we spoke with Father Yu'annis, a couple went to the granite bowl that Mary had used to prepare dough. They devoutly touched the bowl, put their hands in the water in the bowl, and brought this to their mouths. "Is this water from the well?" I asked. "No," Father Yu'annis said, "it is tap water put there to prevent people from putting money inside. Because the bowl is open, the money attracted less spiritual people to steal it. With the water there, people don't place money in the bowl any more."

"But these people apparently believe this water is blessed?" I asked. "Let them take the water and do with it according to their faith," the priest responded. "It depends on one's faith."

Samannud is a site on the Holy Family's route where hardly any Christians live. In Samannud itself, perhaps twenty or thirty Christian families remain. Most Christians have left for nearby Mahallat al-Kubra or other cities. Yet there are always many faithful in the church who have come from different parts of the Delta, Cairo, and, during the feast days of Apa Anub, from Upper Egypt. They know about the Holy Family, and they know of the blessing of the well, but asking Apa Anub for intercession is clearly the most important reason for pilgrimage.

Al-Burullus

According to the homily of Zacharias, the Holy Family traveled north to al-Burullus, an area full of salt marshes, near the Lake of al-Burullus, which was a good place to hide from the soldiers of Herod. There is no archaeological evidence from those days. The marshes have been cultivated, and only the lake remains.

In the area of al-Burullus was a group of four

monasteries. One of them is the Monastery of Dimyana, ten kilometers north of Bilqas. Another was perhaps Dayr al-Maghtis, or Dabra Metmaq, which played an important role in the Coptic Orthodox Church in the Middle Ages. Dayr al-Maghtis was destroyed by a great fire in the year 1438. The other two monasteries were those of al-'Askar and al-Maymana, but neither has survived.

The Convent of Saint Dimyana near Bilqas stands alone in the fields.

Dimyana

If the Holy Family passed through al-Burullus, they could also have passed through Dimyana, which is often described as 'the wilderness of Bilqas,' in reference to the salt marshes for which the area was once known.

Today Dimyana is a mixed Christian–Muslim village with a convent built on a spot where local Christians believe the Holy Family rested. That place was chosen by Saint Dimyana to worship God, and she was martyred there, along with forty virgins. Coptic Christians believe that the convent was built by Dimyana's father. Others say her tomb was built in the fourth century by Saint Helena, but nothing has remained of that period.

Medieval manuscripts do not mention Dimyana as one of the locations the Holy Family visited, but according to Father Hadra of the village of Dimyana, the story is based on

Facing page:
A priest lights a candle before the icon of Saint Dimyana near Bilqas.

A priest walks through the old Church of St. Dimyana near Bilqas.

ancient oral traditions. Educated Christians in Cairo are more skeptical and believe this is a later development in the tradition of the path of the Holy Family. Whatever the answer is, the oral tradition does not contradict what is reported in medieval manuscripts.

Bikha Isous

The Holy Family traveled westward and came to the place now known by the name of Sakha, a town 135 kilometers north of Cairo. "When the Holy Family arrived they were thirsty, but found no water," Father Tadrus, who received us in the church, says. "But then the child Jesus touched a stone with his foot, water spouted forth, and his foot left an imprint."

Father Tadrus says this place therefore became known as Bikha Isous, which means 'the footprint of Jesus.' "The stone with the imprint of Jesus' foot was later found in Dayr al-Maghtis, which means 'monastery of the pool.' It was called that because it was well known as a place where people went for baptisms. Also, Saint Dimyana went there to be baptized. When the monastery was destroyed in the thirteenth century, one of the monks took the stone and hid it under the ground in front of the door of the monastery."

Little archaeological evidence, if any, remains to indicate where exactly the monastery was located. This led the well-known researcher in Coptic Church history Otto Meinardus to conclude in 1977 that he was unable to locate this place. But some people believe the name Sakha could be a permutation of the name Bikha, because the names look similar if the diacritical points are omitted in Arabic.[9]

The Discovery of Bikha Isous

Traditions develop, and so did the tradition of the Holy Family with the discovery of Bikha Isous. Father Matthias Maurice says the stone with the footprint of Jesus was discovered in April 1984.

Workers were digging a hole for sewage in the unpaved street leading to the entrance of the church in Sakha. At a depth of approximately 1.5 meters, the workers found a light gray stone about eighty centimeters long with a little brownish dent, which people believed was the footprint of a two- or three-year-old child. On the back of the same stone the word *Allah* (God) was written in Arabic. On top of that stone they found another one that resembled half a capital from a column. Halim Philippus Mikha'il, at the time of the discovery a supervisor in a factory and still a member of the church council in Sakha, immediately cried out, "This is the footprint of Jesus!" Halim knew that according to tradition the monks who had buried the stone of Bikha Isous had placed half the crown of a column as a marker on top of it. Halim shouted in excitement, "I jumped in the hole and drank its ground water, for it was holy water. Others joined me, and it was a real joy when we discovered the stone."

With the discovery of the stone, miracles occurred. "A beautiful odor came from this stone," says Halim, and Father Matthias relates that "a man with an eye disease washed his eyes in the water, and his disease was healed."

At the time of the discovery, Father Thomas al-Baramusi and Father Matthias were serving the church. Metropolitan Bishoi, to whose bishopric Sakha belongs, and Pope Shenuda had been under arrest in their monastery since September 1981, when the late President Sadat had arrested hundreds of Christian and Muslim leaders. Both Pope Shenuda and Metropolitan Bishoi were set free for Coptic Christmas on January 6, 1985. This arrest made the priests of Sakha decide to bring the stone to Pope Shenuda in the Monastery of Bishoi. "Pope Shenuda kept the stone for some time. He prayed and made three liturgies over the stone, and then told us this really was the stone of Bikha Isous that is mentioned in our tradition," says Father Matthias. "The miracles and the

The Church of the Holy Virgin at Sakha, where the stone with Jesus' footprint (Bikha Isous) was discovered in 1985.

prayers of Pope Shenuda convinced us this was the stone on which Jesus left his foot imprint."

Father Matthias showed us the back of the stone, which has the word *Allah* written in Arabic, followed by a vertical line. Father Matthias says this text must have been written by one of the monks in the Middle Ages. "The vertical line following the word 'Allah' could be explained as the number one, and thus the text could read 'one God,' and we believe in one God," says Father Matthias. "Another explanation is that it is an *alif* [the first letter of the Arabic alphabet], which could be an abbreviation of *ibn*, which means 'son,' and thus the text could mean 'son of God,' in reference to Jesus."

Western scholars such as Otto Meinardus, however, are not convinced that the stone bears the footprint of Jesus. Meinardus wrote in his recent book *Two Thousand Years of Coptic Christianity* that he has still been unable to find the location of Bikha Isous.[10] But Father Matthias is not at all deterred that Western scholars are not convinced. "We have faith that this stone is indeed the footprint of Jesus," he says.

The two statements show a difference in culture, with different starting points. Western scholars do not believe until they have something proved, while the Coptic Orthodox tradition starts by believing and needs to have something disproved. In this context, Western tradition attaches great value to scholarly evidence and makes Westerners skeptical about a certain belief if no convincing evidence can be provided. On the other hand, the Coptic Orthodox tradition attaches great value to faith and the statements or revelations of important church fathers, who would not make such statements if they were not supported by known facts and tradition. Thus the logic that 'it is true if we have evidence' stands diametrically opposed to the reasoning that 'it is true if it comes from a trusted source and it could be true.'

Since it was discovered, the stone has become an important destination for pilgrimage. It has been placed in a glass case in the back of the church. People pray there and put little pieces of paper in the case with their prayers, requests for blessings, or a few words of thanksgiving on them. On the first day of June, the day the church celebrates the arrival of the Holy Family in Egypt, the stone is carried by Metropolitan Bishoi in a procession in a liturgy around the church, and holy oil is put on the footprint.

The church in Sakha has prepared itself for a growing number of pilgrims. Above the entrance of the church is a recent painting of Mary sitting with the Christ Child on a donkey and Joseph walking beside it. The addition of this painting demonstrates that the church deliberately wants to be connected to the story of the Holy Family in Egypt. Father Matthias accentuates that by saying, "In our history, visiting Sakha or Bikha Isous was considered to be equal to visiting Jerusalem."

Wadi al-Natrun

The Holy Family went farther west and crossed the Nile. According to some accounts, the Holy Family saw Wadi al-Natrun, about halfway between Cairo and Alexandria, from afar and blessed it, but others say the family visited the area. Father Matthias from Sakha does not know, but he is certain Mary blessed this place "because she knew that this place would become a place for serving God."

On the way from the Delta to Wadi al-Natrun, Jesus created a well in the village of al-Hamra, which is still called Bir Maria today. The well had been neglected for many years, but is now being restored.

Wadi al-Natrun is the most important monastic center in Egypt. The area is full of ruins of monasteries and caves where the early hermits lived. Today four large monasteries remain: Macarius (Abu Maqar), Bishoi, al-Suryan, and Baramous.

Nikiou

According to tradition the Holy Family stayed for seven days in the city of Nikiou, where Jesus

healed a man who was possessed.[11] But today Nikiou seems to be forgotten. It is not on the official list of sites of the Holy Family of the Coptic Orthodox Church. The town does not exist any more and it is not even certain where exactly the ruins of Nikiou are located. Father Shenuda Sadiq 'Ayyad of Tanta, a member of the Holy Family Committee of the Coptic Orthodox Church, explains that there are ruins at two different locations that are both called Nikiou; Nikiou the Great near Zawyat Razin, eight kilometers south of Minuf, and Nikiou the Small, eighteen kilometers northwest of Tanta. Father Shenuda does not know the tradition Randal Stewart refers to in the Coptic Encyclopedia, but "we know the Holy Family was in Sakha and went along the Western Desert to Cairo. They may have passed Nikiou the Great but not Nikiou the Small. We are not sure about this."[12]

Dayr Anba Bishoi in Wadi al-Natrun.

A monk near the old wall of Dayr Anba Bishoi.

The Monastery of the
Holy Virgin, also known
as Dayr al-Suryan
(Monastery of the Syrians),
Wadi al-Natrun.

Monks speaking together in
the shadows of the walls inside
Dayr al-Baramous.

Crosses placed in the desert by pilgrims to Wadi al-Natrun.

Pilgrims crowding into the Church of the Holy Virgin, inside Dayr al-Baramous. The church has elements from different periods, some as old as the ninth century. The icon at right is of Saint Moses the Black.

A nineteenth-century photograph of the obelisk from the site that was known as the city of On. Photograph by Hippolyte Arnoux, courtesy of the Schrafberg collection.

Cairo

The Holy Family went to 'Ayn Shams (today a northern suburb of Cairo), which in the Old Testament is called On or Beth-shemesh, the 'house of the sun' (Jer. 43:13).[13] The local inhabitants refused to welcome and host the Holy Family, who went on to Matariya.

Matariya

In Matariya the Holy Family found shade under a sycamore tree. At that spot Jesus created a well, blessed it, and drank from it. Mary also used the water of the well to bathe Jesus. On the place where she poured the water grew a balsam tree, which gave a beautiful odor. This plant is still used today for different types of perfume. The plant is also used for the preparation of the chrism or holy myron, which is holy oil that has been consecrated since apostolic times. From generation to generation, a little of the old oil is added to the new, which has carried the blessing from the earliest days of the church until the present.

The current tree may be only one hundred years old, but belief holds that it came from an offshoot of a tree that grew there in 1672, which in turn was from another offshoot, and so the history of the tree is said to go back for two thousand years.

In recent years many efforts have been made to save the tree from the encroaching city. Pope Shenuda visited the tree in 1979 and asked for special care for it. On January 5, 1986, Mahir

A Muslim and a Christian girl from Upper Egypt standing together underneath the Tree of the Holy Virgin. The tree is believed to have provided shade for the Holy Family at Matariya

'Ayyad wrote an article in *Watani*, a Christian weekly, under the title "Save the Tree of Matariya." Efforts were undertaken, but most important was the establishment in 1999 of the National Egyptian Heritage Revival Association (NEHRA), which has made a serious effort to save the tree of Matariya and other sites related to the Holy Family.

Everything in the immediate area of the tree is named after Mary. There is a Saint Mary's Church (Catholic), a Mosque of the Tree of Mary, Mary's Well, and even Mary's Housing Blocks. Today the site is a popular destination for Muslim and Christian visitors who hold Mary in high esteem.

Zaytun

Until recently, Zaytun, a quarter in Cairo, was not mentioned as a site on the Holy Family's route, but since the apparition of the Holy Virgin there in 1968 many people believe that the Holy Family must have visited this location.

Klot Bek and Anba Ruways

At Klot Bek, the Holy Family is said to have blessed the well of a farmer who gave them water and melons. Today one finds in this location a residence for monks of Dayr al-Suryan. Father Rufa'il al-Suryani, who takes care of the prayer place, says a guide at the Coptic museum stated that the monks' residence stands on the place where a fourth-century church once stood. The well at the entrance of the residence is no longer used for drinking, but only for baptism.

Beside the prayer place one finds the large church of Saint Mark of Azbakiya, which housed the Coptic Orthodox patriarchate from the 1850s until 1968, when the new patriarchate was inaugurated at Anba Ruways in 'Abbasiya.

In front of the papal residence in Anba Ruways stands an old medieval church, which, some people say, is also one of the places the Holy Family passed through. In this way, all churches in Cairo that once functioned as a patriarchate have some link to a site the Holy Family visited.

A woman holds a
lit candle before an
icon of the Holy
Virgin in the Church
of the Holy Virgin
at Zaytun.

Bishops celebrating Christmas at the Cathedral of Saint Mark at Anba Ruways, 'Abbasiya.

Pope Shenuda III presiding over Christmas celebrations at the Cathedral of Saint Mark at Anba Ruways, 'Abbasiya.

Harat Zuwayla

The next location on the itinerary is the Church of the Holy Virgin of Harat Zuwayla in the district of al-Khurinfish, near al-Muski.

At the entrance of the church, which is now part of a convent, one finds a late-nineteenth-century icon of the flight into Egypt. Near the altar is a sacred well, which is believed to have been blessed by the Holy Family and whose waters cure illnesses. Not much remains of the well, which is covered with a few stones. Since the High Dam was built in the 1960s, the ground water in Cairo has been rising and is damaging the foundations of buildings such a the churches in Old Cairo and the Church of the Holy Virgin of Harat Zuwayla, which is seven meters below ground level. Pumps run day and night to keep the historic church dry.

Babylon

The Holy Family stayed a few days in Babylon, which is now part of Old Cairo. Girgis Daoud, librarian of the Coptic Orthodox Seminary, however, believes they could not have stayed in Babylon on their way to Upper Egypt because Babylon was a Roman garrison, and Herod could have asked to have them arrested. He firmly believes, though, that the Holy Family stayed in Babylon on their return home, because Herod had now died.[14]

Babylon is special among the holy places in Cairo because tradition says the Holy Family did not just pass by; rather, they stayed here for a few days, as they did in Musturud, Sakha, Samannud, and Tell Basta. Tradition also relates that the Holy Family stayed for a few days in the crypt in Babylon. Later, the Church of Abu Sarga was built on this location, giving this church an extra blessing.

That Babylon was a stop on the Holy Family's route is evident, many of Egypt's Christians believe, because the place became an important center of Christian life with many churches. This blessing throughout history is in itself seen as a confirmation that the Holy Family must have stopped at this location.

Ma'adi

The next location on the official southward itinerary of the church is Ma'adi, ten kilometers south of Old Cairo, where the Holy Family took a boat to sail to Upper Egypt, in order to stay out of the hands of the pursuing soldiers. According to Father Antonius of the Holy Virgin Church of Ma'adi, Joseph could finance the travel by boat thanks to the gold, frankincense, and myrrh that the wise men had presented to Jesus (Matt. 2:11). Father Antonius believes his church stands on the place of a synagogue that was used during a time when some Jews had fled to Egypt for refuge (Jer. 41:16–18, 42–44).

As at other holy sites, the church in Ma'adi also boasts important miracles. One tradition reports that the fourteenth-century saint Barsum the Naked once healed a young man and ordered him to go to the church in Ma'adi to kiss the steps leading to the waters of the Nile and submerge himself three times in the water in front of the church, just as the prophet Elisha asked Naaman to wash himself in the river Jordan (2 Kings: 5). Miracles are often seen in retrospect as proof that the Holy Family must have passed by and blessed a location. How else could it be that the miracle took place just at that spot and not somewhere else?

Another miracle is from a more recent date. On Friday, Baramhat 3, A.M. 1692 (March 12, 1976), a deacon found a Holy Bible floating on the water. The Bible was open to the chapter of Isaiah 19, which contains the words "blessed be Egypt My people." This Bible is on display in a room on the left side of the church, together with a number of important icons. One must remove one's shoes before entering this holy place, just as Moses was told to do before the burning bush (Exod. 3:5), for the place is holy ground. The room is often packed with people who come for prayer.

In addition to the steps leading to the Nile, the Bible open to Isaiah 19, and the monumental church with its characteristic three cupolas, one also finds an ancient vault, through which monks escaped to the Nile in times of attacks on the church.

Entrance to the Convent of the Holy Virgin at Harat Zuwayla, Cairo.

Following pages: Crosses on tombs in the Coptic Orthodox cemetery in Old Cairo.

The interior and altar of the Church of Saints Sergius and Bacchus, Babylon, Old Cairo.

A Byzantine column in the Church of the Holy Virgin (al-Damshiriya), Old Cairo.

The Church of the Holy Virgin, also known as the Hanging Church, Old Cairo.

Facing page: The Church of the Holy Virgin, also known as Qasriyat al-Rihan, Babylon.

Coptic Orthodox Easter
celebration at the Church
of Saint Barbara, Babylon,
Old Cairo.

The Church of the Holy
Virgin at Ma'adi, where
the Holy Family traditionally embarked by boat to
Upper Egypt, as seen
from the Nile.

A priest on the steps
leading from the Church
of the Holy Virgin at
Ma'adi to the Nile, from
where the Holy Family
traditionally departed for
Upper Egypt.

Facing page:
The main path in
Babylon, Old Cairo.

Traveling Farther South

According to many accounts, the Holy Family went south by boat. But, says Father Matta Salib of the Monastery of Abu Sayfayn at Tammua, eleven kilometers south of Giza, the Holy Family first traveled through an ancient tunnel under the Nile to the location of his monastery, and from there they set out on a boat headed to Upper Egpyt.[15] Father Matta's story is not widely supported, but that does not shake his belief, because he says the visit of the Holy Family to Tammua was revealed in a dream to Pope Cyril VI (1959–71). The church was extended in this century and not much remains to be seen of the old structure. Even the *qasr* (keep) has disappeared.

Maurice Martin mentions that in the sixth century, Christians in a village near Memphis claimed their ancestors gave shelter to the Holy Family on their flight to Egypt, but today no remains can be found.[16] Yet Memphis is not entirely forgotten in the tradition of the Holy Family. Bishop Philippus links Memphis to the prophecies of Isaiah 19:13 ("the leaders of Memphis are deceived") and Jeremiah 2:16 ("the men of Memphis").[17]

Medieval manuscripts mention Dayr al-Muharraqa, south of the pyramid of Lisht between Dahshur and Maydum on the west bank of the Nile, in lists of places sanctified by the Holy Family.[18] But Dayr al-Muharraqa has disappeared. A village of the same name had its name changed in 1939 to Sa'udiya. Some Muslim villagers showed us the funerary temple of the pyramid of al-Muharraq, which they thought may once have been used as a church. No Christians live in Sa'udiya, but Christians in neighboring villages were not aware of the tradition of the Holy Family visiting their area.

Twenty-five kilometers north of Beni Suef, on the east bank of the Nile, is a village with a population that is 90 percent Christian. It is called Dayr ('monastery of') al-Maymun, because it was once a monastic settlement. Villagers believe that when the Holy Family sailed south, they passed their village and Jesus blessed the place. Later, Saint Anthony lived there, and a monastery was built.

The next location visited was the village of Ihnasiya, sixteen kilometers west of Beni Suef. Al-Maqrizi, a fifteenth-century Muslim historian, mentions that the Holy Family rested in Ihnasya under a palm tree, which bent before Jesus when he wanted to eat some of its fruit. Local Muslims did not know the story of the Holy Family in their village, but were quick to bring us to Father Ilyas Rashid. Father Ilyas is certain that the Holy Family visited Ihnasya and suspects "it may have been on the location of the old church of Ihnasya, which collapsed seven hundred years ago during an earthquake that brought the entire village under the earth." Only recently a new church was built, but this building has no relation to the Holy Family, the priest explains.

Ishnin al-Nasara

Perhaps twelve kilometers southwest of Maghagha is Ishnin al-Nasara. Magdi Furuq Hanna, a primary-school teacher and head of the social programs of the church, says that "when Mary and Jesus came to Ishnin al-Nasara, Jesus felt very thirsty. They saw the well, forty-five meters deep, but it was empty and Jesus cried. The Holy Virgin took his finger and held it over the well. The well immediately produced water that rose to the top so the Holy Family could drink. After they had drunk enough, the water fell back to a very low level. Since the Holy Family drank from this well, the water rises every year on August 21 at around 4:00 P.M. Pilgrims who have come to the church for that occasion can drink from its water." Father Yu'annis, who later joined the conversation, added that the water sometimes rises on August 22.

Christians believe Ishnin al-Nasara is on the route of the Holy Family but, says Father

A nineteenth-century
albumen print of the altar
in the Church of Saints
Sergius and Bacchus,
Babylon, Old Cairo.
Courtesy of the
Schrafberg collection.

The Step Pyramid of Pharaoh Zoser at Saqqara, near Memphis where the Holy Family is believed to have stayed.

Above right:
The churches of Abu Sayfayn and Saint Anthony in the village of Dayr al-Maymun. Local tradition says that as Jesus passed this site by boat, he gave it his blessing.

Ruins of the funerary temple of the pyramid
of Dayr al-Muharraqa, located between Dahshur
and Maydum, which may once have been
used as a church. The hill in the background is
all that is left of the pyramid.

A villager rests at
the door of the
Church of Abu
Sayfayn in Dayr
al-Maymun

Sunset over the Church of St. George at Ishnin al-Nasara, where tradition says Jesus came and drank from the well.

The Church of the Holy Virgin in the Christian village of Dayr al-Garnus, where it is believed the Holy Family stayed during their journey.

Yu'annis, "the main celebration is a *nahda* to commemorate Father Mikha'il al-Beheri, whose relics are kept in the church."[19]

Magdi Faruq Hanna estimates the present church to be perhaps one thousand years old. "In 1945 cracks appeared in the church, and they wanted to tear it down and build a new one. Each time they built new walls, a crack appeared in them, until Saint George came to someone in a dream and said 'I didn't want to leave my place. I want to stay in my own church.' After that they decided to restore and paint it," Magdi says.

Dayr al-Garnus

Dayr al-Garnus, today a Christian village with some ten thousand inhabitants, is approximately ten kilometers west of Ishnin al-Nasara and eight kilometers north of al-Bahnasa. It is believed to be a site where the Holy Family rested on their way to al-Ashmunayn. Inhabitants of Dayr al-Garnus noted that their village was distinguished from Ishnin al-Nasara by the fact that the Holy Family spent a few days in Dayr al-Garnus but only passed through Ishnin al-Nasara. "The place the Holy Family stayed," Father Shenuda of Dayr al-Garnus says, "later became known as Pei-Isus [in Coptic] or Bayt Isus or Dayr Bisus, that is to say, 'house of Jesus.'"[20]

The story of the Holy Family in Dayr al-Garnus is closely interwoven with that of Ishnin al-Nasara and al-Bahnasa.

"Al-Bahnasa became known for its many monasteries and monks. Dayr Isus was one of these monasteries, but when the monks disappeared it became a Christian village that has, over the centuries, had its name corrupted to Dayr al-Garnus," Father Shenuda says. He continues, "This church was once the residence of the bishop of the monastery. With the exception of the altar in our church, nothing else remains of the monastery of that time."

Father Shenuda says that the Synaxarium indicates that al-Bahnasa already had a bishop in the fourth century. "One of al-Bahnasa's best-known bishops was Bishop Cyriacus, who lived in the seventh century.[21] He wrote about the discovery of a manuscript by Saint Joseph the Carpenter, in which he wrote that the Holy Family stayed four days in Dayr al-Garnus," says Father Shenuda. He adds that the manuscript of Joseph had been lost.

Nashaat Zaklama, however, does not mention a manuscript from Joseph, but writes that Bishop Cyriacus based his account on Father Antonius, who witnessed a miraculous light on a hill with a tomb. Father Antonius was told in a vision that this was the place the son of God had visited together with his mother, Joseph, and their servant girl Salome. So Father Antonius went to the place and read the Gospel of Saint John. The Holy Virgin appeared to him with her son, who said, "This is the altar of glory I placed here until the end of generations . . . even if the place is desolate, it will be remembered forever." Bishop Cyriacus recorded what Father Antonius had told him, then wrote, "We spent all night praying together for God to reveal to us the mystery of that holy place." The Holy Virgin also appeared to Bishop Cyriacus and confirmed what she had previously told Father Antonius.[22]

The present Church of the Holy Virgin in Dayr al-Garnus was built on the place where the miraculous light had been. The most important site in the church is an ancient well. Meinardus does not doubt that the well once functioned as a Nilometer, measuring the height of the river's flood. For centuries the church has been celebrating a prayer at the well on Bashans 24 (June 1). "That is when we celebrate the arrival of the Holy Family to Dayr al-Garnus," Father Shenuda says.

The current church building, according to Father Shenuda, dates from only 1924, but it was built on the site of a seventeenth-century church, which in turn was built in place of a seventh-century church. The iconostasis is dated to 1591. Father Shenuda says the Holy Virgin appeared to show people where to find the stones for the building of a new church. Magdi, a deacon, claims, however, that the Virgin appeared to Father Yuhanna al-Shuwayli, the priest of the church at that time. "He was fast asleep when the Holy Virgin appeared to him and told him to build a new church, but he was angry because there was no money and there were no bricks, but after the Holy Virgin had taken him to a tree that, with its offshoots throughout the centuries, had possibly been there for two thousand years, he started believing and began, in faith, building a new church."

As with other locations the Holy Family visited, Dayr al-Garnus became a blessing for many people who came there in faith. "In the area around the well, no one is stung by a scorpion or bitten by a snake," says Father Shenuda. And Magdi adds: "Many miracles have happened here. In 1983 two workers in the church fell down from a height of seven or eight meters. The believer of the two just had some scratches on his hands, but the other man was seriously injured."

Many pilgrims come during the ceremony of the well on June 1, but most pilgrims are seen during the Feast of the Holy Virgin on August 21. "We guess we have some thirty to fifty thousand visitors on that day," Father Shenuda says.

It is remarkable that Christians in Dayr al-Garnus say that the water in the well in their vil-

An arch of the church in the ruins beneath a Muslim cemetery at al-Bahnasa.

lage rises on June 1, while the Christians in neighboring Ishnin al-Nasara say this happens in their well on August 21 or 22. But Father Yu'annis of Ishnin al-Nasara does not believe this is strange. "Perhaps the Holy Family blessed the well of Dayr al-Garnus on June 1 while they blessed the well at Ishnin al-Nasara on their return to Palestine on August 21 or 22."

Al-Bahnasa (Oxyrhynchus)

Al-Bahnasa, seventeen kilometers west of the town of Bani Mazar and eight kilometers southeast of Dayr al-Garnus, must have been an important city, but if one looks for the remains

A well situated below a tree that tradition says Jesus planted from a piece of wood, at al-Bahnasa.

of that great history one is bound to be disappointed. The only thing remaining is a well and a tree in the middle of a desolate Muslim cemetery.

"When the child Jesus played near the well, he planted a piece of wood in the soil that grew into a green and fruitful tree," Abu Sayfayn, the brother of Father Shenuda of Dayr al-Garnus, says. "Christians do come here for visits, but not very many."

Today no Christians live in al-Bahnasa, but they live in its twin village, Sandafa, which has a church dedicated to St. George, built in 1923. In 1995 archaeologists found the remains of a church beneath a Muslim cemetery of al-Bahnasa, one of the few remains of the town's Christian history. Abu Sayfayn says Christians in the area believe this church is one of the 366 churches that were once in this area. The others must still be buried.

Gabal al-Tayr

The next destination was Gabal al-Tayr, which is Arabic for 'Mount of the Birds,' so named because migratory birds would rest on the top of it. According to some accounts, the Holy Family first went to Samalut, where they crossed the Nile to Gabal al-Tayr. According to other accounts, they crossed the Nile from west to east at al-Qays (Cynopolis), then traveled thirty-five kilometers south to Gabal al-Tayr.

For many centuries pilgrims would first travel to Bani Khalid, two kilometers south of Samalut, where a ferry crosses the Nile, then climb the 166 steps leading to the top of the cliff. The ferry and stairs are still there, but the government has built an eastern desert road from Cairo to Minya, a branch of which leads to Gabal al-Tayr. Most pilgrims now take the easier route by bus over the eastern desert road and do not cross the Nile anymore.

When we came to visit the church, Father Matta blessed two Muslim men and two Muslim women wearing headscarves. One man and woman had just been married and asked the priest to pray for them to receive a child. The others were a brother and sister who came to ask the priest for a prayer to find a suitable bridegroom for the woman. Father Matta told us that both Christians and Muslims frequently come to this place for a blessing.

Father Matta says that "when the boat of the Holy Family approached the cliff, a piece of rock fell off and would have fallen on the boat had Jesus not lifted his hand and protected the Holy Family. His hand left an imprint on the rock, and this is why the mountain is also called Gabal al-Kaff, or 'mountain of the palm.'"

The Nile no longer flows immediately below the cliff, but with the steep cliff still present, one can imagine the enormous miracle of the three-year-old child stopping a rock from falling on the boat.

Another account of why the mountain is called Gabal al-Kaff says that in the time of the Holy Family's visit, a pharaonic temple stood on the place where the church is today. When the Holy Family approached, the idols in this temple collapsed, which made the priests angry, and they tried to chase the Holy Family out. When this happened, the Holy Family stood to one side, against the mountain, with the Nile on their other side. In that moment Jesus put his hand on the mountain and made it split in two. They entered the cleft, where they could hide from the angry priests. That is why an imprint of Jesus' hand was left on the rock, and the cleft of Mary can be found.[23]

The rock with the imprint of Jesus' hand has been lost. Bishop Paphnutius of Samalut says there are many different versions of what happened to the rock. "According to one story, it lies buried in the silt of the Nile. Another holds that it was taken to Jerusalem by a king who wanted to hold an exhibition of relics of the Holy Family. A third account relates that Salah al-Din carried it off during the Crusades and stowed it in some unknown place."

According to Father Matta of Gabal al-Tayr, Father Shenuda Sadiq 'Ayyad of Tanta has seen the rock in the British Museum.

Father Shenuda says, "In September 1986, I was with my wife and children in the British Museum, where I saw a stone measuring about 40 centimeters by 30 centimeters, with the imprint of three fingers and a palm. On a text beside it was written, 'this is the handprint of Jesus, according to the Coptic folk tradition.' After I returned to Egypt I told the late Bishop Yu'annis of Gharbia, who had an interest in archaeology, what I had seen, but the bishop said we cannot prove this is the stone of the handprint of Jesus." [24]

Today one finds the Church of the Holy Virgin, which was once part of a monastery, on top of the cliff. The monastery disappeared in the second half of the nineteenth century, but its name, Dayr al-'Adhrâ' (Monastery of the Virgin), and the ancient church remained.

A priest walks up
the stairs leading to
Gabal al-Tayr from
the Nile Valley.

The Church of the Holy Virgin on top of the cliff at Gabal al-Tayr.

The Nile Valley, looking south from Gabal al-Tayr.

Facing page: The view from the Nile Valley, looking up at the dwellings used by pilgrims during celebrations at Gabal al-Tayr.

A sign on the western wall of the church, posted by the Egyptian Organization for Antiquities, says the church was founded by Helena, the mother of Constantine, the first Christian emperor, in the year A.M. 44 (A.D. 328), but the Coptic Encyclopedia makes no reference to Saint Helena's alleged instruction to found the church.

Next to the ancient church, Bishop Paphnutius built a bishop's residence. Nearby the church is a small Christian village. Residents earn their income from masonry and pilgrims. Outside the pilgrimage season many houses are empty, but during the season, in the first week of June and the Feast of the Holy Virgin in August, tens of thousands of pilgrims come and hardly any free space can be found.

From the square in front of the church, one has an absolutely marvelous view of the Nile flowing graciously through the green valley. Not far from the church are the stairs down the cliff to the road to Minya. Just two kilometers down the road stood Shagarat al-'Abid, the worshiping tree, which, local people believe, bowed to Jesus when he passed by on his way to al-Ashmunayn. The tree was first described by Father Samuel (later Bishop Samuel) in the mid-1980s. In January 2001, rumors were spread that local government officials wanted to regulate visitation to this site by building a walled enclosure for the tree. Local farmers seem to have perceived this as a threat to their property and removed the tree before intervention was possible—a move highly regretted by church officials.

A priest walks behind columns in the Church of the Holy Virgin at Gabal al-Tayr.

The Worshiping Tree, where
the Holy Family is said to have
passed by on their way to
al-Ashmunayn. The branches
crawled along the ground,
giving the tree its name.

The Church of Apa Hor at Sawada on the east bank of the Nile south of Minya, where local tradition says the Holy Family passed. The church is named after a third-century martyr.

Minya and Bani Hasan

At the foot of the great Christian necropolis of Minya at Sawada on the east bank of the Nile, four kilometers south of the town of Minya, is the Church of Apa Hor, a third-century martyr.

Father Apa Hor, who leads this church today, and local parishioners are convinced the Holy Family must have passed their church as well. Bishop Arsanius, however, is less certain: "It is possible, but we have no evidence from any of the manuscripts that refer to the Holy Family."

The belief that the Holy Family visited this location is clearly a local tradition. Its relation to the flight through Egypt may be weak, but the ancient church certainly deserves a visit. Like the one at Gabal al-Tayr, the Church of Apa Hor is cut into the rock. One enters the nave through a narrow tunnel, which has empty tombs on both sides. Worshipers now place their shoes in the tombs while they pray. To the left inside the church is a well, which is apparently no longer used. Above the cave church of Apa Hor is the Church of Saint Dimyana, which is from a much later date.

Bishop Demetrius of Mallawi writes in his booklet "The Visit of the Holy Family to

Mallawi" that the Holy Family also visited Bani Hasan, where the famous pharaonic tombs of the Eleventh and Twelfth Dynasties are found, but most texts on the Holy Family omit Bani Hasan. Many of these tombs were inhabited by Christian anchorites from the fourth through sixth centuries. This is evident from the Christian graffiti dating from this period in several of these tombs.

Early Christian inscriptions dating to between the fourth and the sixth centuries inside tomb number 23, the tomb of Nouternekht.

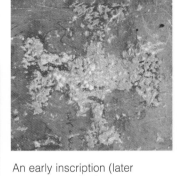

An early inscription (later chipped away) of a cross inside the tomb of Nouternekht at Bani Hasan.

Parishioners parading new icons around the Church of Apa Hor after mass.

One of the pharaonic tombs at Bani Hasan.

Ancient Greek writing on the agora (marketplace) beside the Corinthian columns at Hermopolis Magna, which shows that the basilica was in the center of this ancient Greek city.

Al-Ashmunayn
(Hermopolis Magna)

According to the official itinerary of the Coptic Orthodox Church, the Holy Family continued from Bani Hasan to Bir al-Sahaba near Shaykh 'Abada, where Jesus made a well. There they crossed the Nile from east to west at al-Roda, continuing to al-Ashmunayn, nine kilometers north of Mallawi. According to tradition, the Holy Family visited both al-Ashmunayn and Mallawi. According to Bishop Demetrius of Mallawi, however, the visit to Bir al-Sahaba comes after the visit to Dayrut Umm Nahla and the city of al-Ashmunayn and Dayrut Umm Nahla.

Today al-Ashmunayn is in ruins. Nearby is a village of the same name; it was probably built upon the extension of the ruins of the once great city of Hermopolis Magna, which was famous in the first centuries after Christ. The name Hermopolis, at least, lives on in the name of the bishopric, which is the bishopric of Mallawi, Hermopolis, and Antinoopolis.

One of the stories told today in relation to al-Ashmunayn is that Jesus raised a person from the dead and a tree that was used to worship Satan bowed its branches to the ground when the Lord passed. Satan was expelled, and the tree became a source of blessing. During the family's wanderings in the city, many idols are said to have

The colossal Corinthian columns of the basilica of Hermopolis (al-Ashmunayn).

A priest blesses two women and a child at Kom Maria just outside the village of Dayr Abu Hinnis, where the Holy Virgin is said to have rested. Women come here to pray for the health of their children.

According to Bishop Demetrius of Mallawi, the Holy Family continued from al-Ashmunayn to Dayrut Umm Nahla, where where the palm trees bowed before Jesus who created a well.[26] Some local people, however, say that the well can be found today in a local mosque. Some Christians say that Muslims changed the name of the well from Bir al-Sahaba (spelled with *sin*; 'well of the cloud') to Bir al-Sahaba (spelled with *sad*, meaning 'well of the Companions [of the Prophet Muhammad]), but others were not aware of this, and local Muslims say not only that there is no mosque of that name but there is no mosque with a well inside the building (although there is one, named after the local Shelayta family, with a well alongside it).

Dayrut Umm Nahla has no church and only a few Christian families. The only reminder in the hands of Christians in Dayrut Umm Nahla is a small exhibition room with some paper statues and articles about the flight to Egypt.

The Holy Family crossed the Nile again from west to east to visit Bir al-Sahaba on the east bank of the Nile, and thus may have landed on the banks of what is today the Muslim village of Shaykh 'Abada.

According to the official itinerary of the Coptic Orthodox Church, the Holy Family crossed the Nile from Dayrut Umm Nahla to Kom Maria at Dayr Abu Hinnis. After that visit, they crossed the Nile again to the west and went to Tell al-Amarna, which has become famous for its ruins of Pharaoh Akhenaten, but no remains of churches are to be seen.

Shaykh 'Abada and Dayr Abu Hinnis

For practical reasons it is easier to combine Shaykh 'Abada, Bir al-Sahaba, Dayr Abu Hinnis, and Kom Maria in one visit because they are all located on the east bank of the Nile.

Just outside the village of Shaykh 'Abada are the ruins of Antinoopolis (in Arabic, Ansina), the capital of the southern Egyptian province of Thebaid,

spontaneously fallen from their plinths and broken. This angered the pagan priests, and the family had to leave the city for their own safety.[25]

The most important ruins in al-Ashmunayn are the colossal Corinthian columns of a basilica that probably date back to the first half of the fifth century. Bishop Demetrius estimates that some 500 Christians live in al-Ashmunayn today. Commercial activities have shifted to the town of Mallawi, which has a relatively wealthy Christian community, among whom the memory of the flight to Egypt is strong.

which flourished in the fourth and fifth centuries.

Muslims in Shaykh 'Abada have only scant knowledge about the Holy Family visiting their area but, says Sayyid Hamdi Khalil, the *'umda* (village head) of Shaykh 'Abada, "Our village is known for the house of Mariam the Copt. She was born and raised here and given as a present by Muqawqas [the ruler of Egypt at the time of the Arab conquest] to the Prophet Muhammad. Her house is visited by both Muslims and Christians. We want to develop this house into a tourist attraction."

Bir al-Sahaba

The Holy Family went from Shaykh 'Abada by land toward the northern part of the Ansina mountains and entered the desert, where Jesus created a well. Radi, a villager from the nearby Christian village of Dayr Abu Hinnis, strongly believes in the miraculous capacity of the twenty-three-meter deep well: "Joseph the Carpenter and the Holy Virgin came to this place but there was no water. Jesus wanted to return to the Nile to get water, but suddenly a large cloud appeared, which provided them with shade against the burning sun, and below that a well sprung up."

Until recently the well was in the middle of the desert, but the Muslim cemetery has been expanding, and for ten to twenty years the well has been surrounded by Muslim tombs. This does not deter Christians, mainly from Dayr Abu Hinnis, from coming here. They come, especially on Fridays, the weekly day off, to pray and to ask for blessings. "In particular, pregnant women and people with diseases come here. They drink from the water, which gives them *baraka*. We know of many miraculous healings after people drank from the well and prayed," says Father Yu'annis Abd al-Masih Tadrus. Radi offered us a cup of water from the well, which tasted excellent.

Bir al-Sahaba, a well said to have been created by Jesus in the desert outside the village of Sheikh 'Abada, known for its baraka (blessing) and for healing the sick. Both Muslims and Christians come to the well to get blessings.

Dayr Abu Hinnis

Dayr Abu Hinnis is a Christian village with some 22,000 inhabitants and three Orthodox and two Evangelical churches. The most important location related to the Holy Family is Kom Maria ('the hill of Maria'), a slightly elevated hill of sand just outside the village, where the Holy Virgin is said to have rested. Kom Maria is less then one kilometer from the ancient church of Abu Hinnis. Most streets in this village are named after saints. The street leading from the church to Kom Maria bears the name 'Street of Saint Maria.'

We walked with Radi and Father Yu'annis to Kom Maria and found on top of the hill two women and a little child called Mary. The two women were the child's aunt and her friend. They were concerned that the child was eighteen months old and still could not walk, so they decided to pray at Kom Maria. Father Yu'annis explains that many people come here for prayer, and Radi tells the story that women who cannot get pregnant go to the top of this hill and " let themselves roll to the foot, after which they will become pregnant."

Kom Maria is usually empty, but on Tuba 3 (January 11 or 12) the church commemorates here the murder of the children of Bethlehem, which marked the beginning of the flight into Egypt (Matt. 2:13–18). Other celebrations are on Bashans 24 (June 1), commemorating the Holy Family crossing the border at al-Arish, and on Ba'una 21 (June 28), the Feast of the Theotokos the Dissolver of the Iron Fetters.[27] On these occasions Bishop Demetrius of Mallawi crosses the Nile from Bayadiya to Dayr Abu Hinnis in a boat decorated with icons of the Holy Family, walks in a procession with icons and singing deacons through the village, and leads thousands of worshipers in their prayers on Kom Maria.

Father Yu'annis explains that the tradition mentions only Kom Maria, but not the land where the Church of Abu Hinnis was later built. "But because our church is located so close to Kom Maria, it is very likely they also passed our church.

They blessed the area, which later became visible in the twelve monasteries that were built in this area and the thousands of monks and hermits who have lived here. The Church of Abu Hinnis was founded by John the Short, who lived in Wadi al-Natrun but who fled to this area in the year 407 after raiders had made the area unsafe."

Father Yu'annis says that many pilgrims have experienced miracles in Dayr Abu Hinnis:

People who are sick or are possessed by an evil spirit come on Fridays, and we pray for them and sometimes miracles happen. Once a woman came with her child. She knew he was sick, but she didn't know what he had. She brought him to the church and explained to me that her child was always quickly frightened. I stood beside the child and asked him to be quiet, but the boy became afraid and started running away. I got him back and after I had said the first words of the prayer "Our Father who art in heaven," the boy fell on the ground and we knew he was possessed by an evil spirit. After the prayer was finished, the child was very quiet and his mother took him home.

The Laura of Dayr Abu Hinnis

The Coptic Orthodox Church has two types of monks: anchorites, or hermits, and cenobites, who live in a monastic community. Sometimes hermits lived in the same general area and formed what was called a *laura*. The remains of a sixth-century *laura* have survived in the mountains near Dayr Abu Hinnis.

The Laura of Dayr Abu Hinnis comprises tens of hermit caves and a rock-cut church in the mountains, dedicated to the Holy Virgin. Villagers believe these places were all blessed by the Holy Family. The hermits prayed, ate, and worked alone in their caves, which generally consisted of one room for living and working and one room for sleeping and prayer. They only met the other brothers during the Divine Liturgy in church.

The church of Saint John the Short at the Christian village of Dayr Abu Hinnis, one of the sites on the traditional route of the Holy Family.

A priest at the altar inside the Church of Saint John the Short at Dayr Abu Hinnis.

A marble stone with Coptic inscriptions on the altar dedicated to the Holy Virgin in the Church of Saint John the Short at Dayr Abu Hinnis.

Facing page: A cross over the entrance of Dayr Abu Sarabam, outside the town of Dayrut

Dayr Abu Sarabam,
outside the town of Dayrut.
The tree hanging over
the wall is believed to have
given shelter to the Holy
Family.

Altar boys recite holy scriptures inside the Church of Abu Sayfayn at Meir. Meir was traditionally blessed by Jesus because the villagers welcomed the Holy Family.

Altar boys pray in the Church of Abu Sayfayn at Meir.

Dayr Abu Sarabam and Dayrut al-Sharif

The Holy Family crossed the Nile again and continued via Tell al-Amarna to Dayrut al-Sharif, where they rested for a few days. Today one finds at this place the Monastery of Abu Sarabam and an old Christian cemetery with a tree that, according to tradition, gave shelter to the Holy Family.

The monastery is taken care of by one monk, Father Bishoi, who says that it dates back to the fourth century. "The monastery is named after Sarabam, bishop of Nikiou, who lived at the end of the third century. Bishop Sarabam escaped the persecution in his city and came to Dayrut."

"The tree in Dayrut is important," says Father Bishoi, "because it provided the Holy Family with shade. The place they passed became holy and later became a church." Today the tree stands in the middle of a centuries-old Christian cemetery. The Christians of Dayrut who were killed by extremists in 1992 are buried at its foot.

"But I don't think the tree is two thousand years old," I ventured. Father Bishoi's response was friendly: "There are people who came from America and Holland who said this tree, which is a casuarina, is two thousand years old. Both Muslims and Christians come here, and are very interested in visiting this place. Muslims come every Friday at noon. They believe in this tree and call it the tree of Mariam. We are Orthodox. We believe in the Bible and the tradition of the fathers. It is just like mathematics. Some things you need to prove, and some axioms are accepted without discussion. We know from the tradition that was delivered to us from generation to generation that the Holy Virgin rested underneath this tree."

Most pilgrims come during their vacations. "Outside the holidays only a few people visit Dayr Abu Sarabam, but during vacations we receive hundreds of visitors per day. We do not encourage pilgrims to come here, but our doors are always open."

Before saying farewell, Father Bishoi plucked a twig from the tree and gave it to us as *baraka*. Some people make tea from it and drink this to cure them from diseases, but, says Father Bishoi "you use it as you believe. This depends on your faith. I will not say how to use it. I will not say you need to drink it or do something else with it."

Al-Qusiya

South of Dayrut lies al-Qusiya. According to tradition, the Holy Family passed through the village of Sanabu, which once had an episcopal see, to al-Qusiya, which in the first century had a temple dedicated to the ancient Egyptian goddess Hathor. Bishop Thomas explains that when the Holy Family arrived in the city the idols fell before Jesus, which made the inhabitants of al-Qusiya chase the Holy Family out of their city: "The only reminder are the ruins of al-Barba, an old pharaonic temple that is said to have been destroyed after Jesus had come to al-Qusiya."

The pagan priests were full of fear for Jesus and told him "Go out of this town lest the children should come out and kill you, since you wish to enter the town in order to destroy it." The Holy Virgin told Pope Theophilus (385–412) in a vision what had happened when they came to al-Qusiya: "And they uttered to us these and similar words, while they, their women and children, and their adults, chased us away." The vision goes on to describe the pain felt by the Holy Family and then states: "My beloved son turned and cursed the town." Jesus said: "Let its people be in an estate lower than all other people, and let them be more lowly and subdued than all the inhabitants of the land of Egypt. Let its earth be cursed so that nothing shall grow in it except [alfalfa] and rush-nut, and let its soil lie uncultivated and remain as it was before I cursed it."[28]

Bishop Gregorius, general bishop for Higher Theological Studies, maintains that the current al-Qusiya cannot be located at the same place as the Qusiya of Jesus' day, because Pope Theophilus wrote that Jesus prophesied that places that refused the Holy Family would be destroyed. The bishop maintains that the cursed Qusiya is five kilometers southeast of the present Qusiya.[29]

Bishop Thomas of al-Qusiya says that the area around the temple of al-Barba had been wasteland until recently. He furthermore says that the story of chasing the Holy Family out "may reflect communal tensions between al-Qusiya and other villages and towns in the time the manuscript was written. I do not believe the people of al-Qusiya chased the Holy Family out, and I do not believe Jesus cursed the town."[30]

Bishop Timotheus, general bishop for al-Qusiya, who works with Bishop Thomas, is equally adamant that Jesus cannot have cursed al-Qusiya, because Jesus said in the Gospel of Luke "Bless them that curse you" [Luke 6:28]. Another indication is that there are no longer areas around al-Qusiya that are either uninhabited or uncultivated. "How then can there be a curse on al-Qusiya?" asks the Bishop.[31]

On the road from al-Qusiya to the Monastery of al-Muharraq lies the village of Sarakna. Some five thousand Christians make up about 90 percent of the population. Father Kirillus of Sarakna knows his village is not on the official itinerary, but "because it is recorded that the Holy Family was in al-Qusiya and in Dayr al-Muharraq, they must have passed through our village as well." Villagers believe that until the 1960s there was a well in the village that had been blessed by the Holy Family, but due to population pressure in the village, the well has been replaced by buildings.

Seven kilometers west of al-Qusiya, not far from Dayr al-Muharraq lies the village of Meir. Unlike Sarakna, Meir is on the official map of the church because it is mentioned in old manuscripts. The inhabitants of Meir welcomed the Holy Family and were blessed with very fertile land and a well.

Father Kirillus went with us to Meir and told us the well has a house built over it, but pilgrims still come to visit it. "Ten years ago I met an Ethiopian monk in Dayr al-Muharraq, Father Pachomius al-Habashi, who revered the well and frequently came here to obtain a blessing."

Father Kirillus also explains that the Church of Abu Sayfayn is perhaps fifty years old. "This church stands on the place where a church was built in 1878, and that one was built over a church from the fourth century. They didn't preserve the old church because they didn't know that later some tourists would come to see it."

"Are there any remains of the first church?" we asked. "Certainly if we dig below this church we will find remains of the first church," Father Kirillus responded after he had spoken to some of the local people, "but there have been no excavations. People from Meir are afraid that if archaeologists start digging, this would impair the worship. They don't want this place to become a place for visitors and not worship."

Miracles are also recorded in Meir. Father Kirillus called over a fifteen-year-old boy called Shenuda, who had fallen from the fourth floor while working on a building. "He was in a coma in a big hospital for five days. He dreamt about saints coming to him and he was cured. He is our miracle."

Shenuda confirms what happened: "I fell from the fourth floor and lost consciousness. I was brought to the hospital, but didn't notice anything. When I woke up I said the name 'Abu Sayfayn.'" Father Kirillus, who was a medical doctor before he became a priest adds, "The doctors said the miracle is not only that he survived, but that he survived without impairment."

The Church of the Holy
Virgin at Dayr al-Muharraq,
which according to Coptic
tradition was founded in
the first century and is the
first church in the world.

The Monastery of the Holy Virgin of al-Muharraq

Twelve kilometers west of al-Qusiya, 327 kilometers south of Cairo, and 48 kilometers north of Asyut lies the Monastery of the Holy Virgin of al-Muharraq, at the foot of the mountains of Qusqam. This monastery is without a doubt the most important location on the Holy Family's itinerary, which makes people sometimes say that a pilgrimage to Dayr al-Muharraq is equal to that of a pilgrimage to Jerusalem (now not permitted, due to church politics). This is the place where according to tradition the Holy Family stayed six months and where Jesus, after the Resurrection, came back to consecrate the altar referred to in Isaiah 19:19 as the "altar to the Lord in the heart of Egypt."

The holiest place in the monastery is the Church of the Holy Virgin. According to tradition, the church contained a well, but it was closed by a former abbot of the monastery for safety reasons. In front of the altar, Father Philoxenos tells the story of the Holy Family:

The story of the Holy Family starts seven hundred years before Christ in the prophecy of Isaiah, which talks about an altar in the middle of Egypt. *This* altar is standing in the middle of the land of Egypt. The prophecy of Isaiah speaks about an altar of the Lord outside Palestine. But the Jews had to worship the Lord in Palestine, and thus Isaiah could not have referred to a Jewish altar. It is a Christian altar. Seven hundred years after this prophecy, the Lord Jesus came here and found shelter in an empty house, which became the last station of the flight of the Holy Family into Egypt, and he sanctified this house and made it a holy place for worshiping the Lord.

The Holy Family, by which I mean the Lord Jesus, the Holy Virgin, Saint Joseph, and Saint Salome, who accompanied them, escaped the soldiers of Herod, who were searching for the child Jesus because they wanted to kill him, after Herod had discovered Jesus had not been among the boys he killed in Bethlehem [Matt. 2:16]. That forced the Holy Family to leave each place they went. But near al-Qusiya a miracle

A monk reads holy texts to a blind deacon in the grounds of Dayr al-Muharraq.

happened. They asked the people of al-Qusiya, "Did you see a Jewish family pass by recently?" The people of al-Qusiya replied, "Yes, but that was when the plants were still little, not grown. The plants have grown now, so it must have been some time ago they were here." The miracle was that God made the plants grow very fast in a short time to make the people believe time had passed faster, so they thought the Holy Family was several months ahead of them, and thus they returned to Herod thinking that they couldn't find them.

Fikri Ramzi and Nashaat Zaklama relate the story of how Yusi, a relative of Mary and Joseph, was told by an angel that he had to travel to Egypt to warn Mary and Joseph that Herod had killed 144,000 children of Bethlehem and that the devil had told Herod where they were hiding.[32] Herod sent ten soldiers to Egypt to bring the Holy Family to him in order to kill the child Jesus with his own hands. Mary cried and wanted to hide in the upper compartment of the house, but Jesus said, "Don't be afraid, don't cry, your crying makes me grieve. The time has not yet come for the Son of Man to be delivered. The soldiers will not find us."

Jesus praised Yusi and told him his reward would be great. Yusi lay down and gave up his spirit, and Joseph and Salome buried him near the house. After that the angels of the Lord appeared to Joseph and told him to return to the land of Israel. Yusi's tomb was discovered on October 12, 2000, during restoration of the ancient church in the monastery. Father Philoxenos says Yusi's remains were found under the threshold of the church, "just as old manuscripts in our monastery described it."

Jesus blessed the house, which later became the church where Yusi was buried, and said:

Everyone who comes to worship in this house I will bestow on him the remission of his sins, if he puts in his heart not to return to them. I will

number him with the saints, and all that are in trouble or afflicted with disease or grief, or any pain and come to this place and asks anything that complies with God's will, I will do everything he asks, and give him all that he wants. For the honor of your holy name, my mother, this place will be a refuge for strangers and a home for

The section of the monastery that houses the monks' cells. Laundry can be seen drying on the roof top; in the background is a Christian cemetery.

saintly monks, which no ruler in this world can harm, because this house has become our refuge.

Also if any barren woman begs with a pure heart and remembers this house, I will give her a seed. Every woman that has difficulty in labor and asks me in your name and remembers your suffering with me will swiftly give birth.[33]

The monks at the monastery pray for Yusi during the Feast of the Cross with the words of Psalms 117 and 118:19–20, and the Gospel of Saint Mark 6:1–6.

Both Fikri Ramzi and Zaklama say Joseph built a house of bricks covered with palm leaves, but Father Philoxenos disagrees with this account:

When the Holy Family came to Dayr al-Muharraq, it was a deserted mud-brick house on the edge of the desert. No one lived in or around the place and thus no one could inform the sol-

Following pages: Dayr al-Muharraq sits in the middle of the Nile Valley surrounded by farms.

diers of Herod. Dayr al-Muharraq means 'the monastery scorched by fire,' in reference to the repeated burning of invasive vegetation, which is an indication that this place was deserted.

Father Philoxenos continued with an explanation of why Dayr al-Muharraq was blessed by the Holy Family more than any other place in Egypt:

The Holy Family stayed here six months and five days, and this was the longest period of time the Holy Family spent in one place in Egypt. An angel of the Lord started them on their journey in Bethlehem by telling them to escape to Egypt, and an angel ended the journey here when he appeared to Saint Joseph and said to go back to Palestine because Herod had died.

This was in the spring of 4 B.C. That is the year Herod died. After the Resurrection, our Lord Jesus came here again, with his disciples and with his mother, to sanctify this place and make it into a church. This is the only place in all the world the Lord Jesus sanctified with his holy hands, and he made three promises for our place.

First, this place will be inhabited until the last day, the day of judgment. This is true because from the first century to the fourth century this place was a church. From the fourth century onward it was a monastery that had been established by the disciples of Father Pachomius, the father of community monasticism in Upper Egypt. We have had periods of weakness for the monasteries in which only a few monks were living here, but this place has never been without

The Bishop gives blessings to monks and pilgrims during the feast of Epiphany in the Church of the Holy Virgin at Dayr al-Muharraq.

A monk passes behind the altar, which according to tradition is the oldest Christian altar in the world, possibly dating back to the first century, although a date inscribed in the marble reads December 11, 747.

monks, and in the last decades we have had many young men who have been called to the monastic life, which brought our number to one hundred. In 1995 Islamic militants killed two monks, and after they did this we consecrated eight new monks. We wanted to say we are going to survive by the power of our Lord Jesus. This place will be inhabited and thriving until the last day of life.

The second promise is that the holy service will be on this altar until the last day of life. This altar is one stone found in this place when our Lord Jesus came here as a child. It was still in its place when he came the second time, after the Resurrection, and he sanctified this stone and it became an altar. We celebrate a daily mass on this altar in the Coptic language, and this is the only church in all of Egypt that still celebrates mass entirely in Coptic.

The third promise is that whoever prays in all sincerity in the Church of the Holy Virgin of the Monastery of al-Muharraq, his or her prayers will be heard.

What is the source for these beliefs? The Bible does not write about these traditions. Father Philoxenos has no difficulty answering this question:

Our belief is based on different traditions. We have the tradition of the Ethiopian church talking about this coming of our Lord Jesus to this place, which they celebrate on the sixth of Hathor, which is the fifteenth of November. On that day we celebrate the consecration of our church by our Lord Jesus, who came here with the twelve disciples—after the disciples had selected Matthias to replace Judas—and his mother, on a cloud, to dedicate the Church of the Holy Virgin in Qusqam Mountain in Dayr al-Muharraq. This is celebrated in both our church and the Ethiopian Church. Also, the Syrian Orthodox Church has a tradition that talks about the visit of our Lord Jesus to this

A Coptic Orthodox liturgical book open in the center of the Church of the Holy Virgin in Dayr al-Muharraq during the feast of Epiphany.

TRACING THE ROUTE OF THE HOLY FAMILY TODAY

place and how he made it holy. Our most important source is Pope Theophilus, the twenty-third pope of Alexandria. He visited this place and wanted to remove this simple house and build a huge cathedral, but the Holy Virgin appeared to him in a vision and told him not to do anything to this simple place, but to leave it as proof of the humble place our Lord Jesus stayed in. We have many manuscripts, and all our liturgical books speak about this visit and Jesus sanctifying this place.

Dayr al-Muharraq was destroyed and rebuilt many times in its long history. No one doubts that the oldest part of the monastery is the Church of the Holy Virgin. Although the monks are certain about the foundation of the church in the first century, Western scholars are not so sure. "Nothing is known for certain about the date of the foundation of this monastery," write Coquin and Martin.[34]

Father Philoxenos is not very impressed by the skepticism of Western scholars:

Not every fact of history is recorded in historical documents. Let's not speak about Theophilus, but consider instead the prophet Isaiah, who wrote about the altar in the midst of Egypt. The proof of Isaiah is stronger than Theophilus. We first depend on the Bible, then we have the doctrines of the apostles, and the third source is the tradition. These are the three sources of faith of the Coptic Orthodox Church. We do not base our belief on Theophilus only, but on Isaiah.

You see, Coptic people are a very religious people. We have a strong belief in the Bible, in the church, the sayings of the church, and the history of the church. We can't deny that there are many stories that are exaggerated. We don't deny this. But we have faith in our church fathers and in what they say. This is a very strong source for the people of Egypt.

The first source we depend on is faith. If historical evidence adds something that confirms it, it is fine, it is acceptable. If it doesn't, it doesn't matter because I already have the faith in my heart.

Father Philoxenos agrees people pick up stories, and a story develops over time, but he says:

I look at whether such a story is a benefit to the faith. If what people believe makes their faith stronger and vital, fine, that is acceptable. But if a certain story contradicts accepted belief and dogma, we must oppose it.

It is thus not a problem if people believe that the locations of their churches—such as Tammua, Apa Hor, and Sarakna—were visited.

It is some kind of spiritual pride and a kind of blessing. They want to be connected to the Holy Family, and that is not a problem, because it is not against the dogma and not against the tradition. Here the people are not so focused on the history but on spiritual things. We are not talking about a research or a PhD on the Holy Family. We are talking about faith, blessings, miracles, about something spiritual. What benefit do we have if we confirm it here and cancel it there? But this is not accepted in the Western world. They ask for documents, proof, and if you don't have proof, it can't be true. That is a different way of thinking.

We thanked Father Philoxenos. During the pilgrimage along the sites of the Holy Family we had been more and more surprised about the many miracles, which often sounded unbelievable to Western ears, but the meeting with Father Philoxenos had made clear that the differences in Coptic and Western thinking were between faith and rationalism. Enriched, we traveled on to the Monastery of the Holy Virgin near Durunka, the southernmost station on the flight of the Holy Family into Egypt.

The Return to Palestine

The Monastery of the Holy Virgin near Durunka

The *Vision of Theophilus* and other manuscripts mention Dayr al-Muharraq as the southernmost point the Holy Family visited, after which they returned north to al-Ashmunayn. In the Vision, the Holy Virgin told Theophilus: "After my Son had spoken thus we rose up and descended from the mountain. We reached the town of Eshmunain and its inhabitants received us with great joy and jubilation. When morning came I carried my Son in my arms, and we came to the sea [i.e., the Nile], where we looked for a ship but found

The cross above the Monastery of the Holy Virgin near Durunka. This is traditionally the southernmost point in the Holy Family's travels in Egypt. From here they returned down the Nile and crossed back into Palestine.

A monk from the Monastery of the Holy Virgin near Durunka lights a candle at the entrance to the cave where apparitions of Saint Mary have appeared in recent years.

none ready. Then my beloved Son made the sign of the Cross on the water and it became like a ship before us. We then went on board and we arrived at Nazareth and gave thanks to God."[35] Nevertheless a tradition has been promoted in the past decades that the Holy Family went from Dayr al-Muharraq approximately fifty kilometers farther south to Durunka. The tradition gained in importance after Bishop Mikha'il of Asyut rebuilt the Church of the Blessed Virgin in the Monastery of the Holy Virgin near Durunka in 1955 and made so many additions that Meinardus, writing originally in 1963, believed that the annual feast between August 7 and 22 would "eventually become the largest Christian *mulid* in Egypt." Meinardus also states that an oral tradition upheld by hundreds of thousands of Copts and supported by Bishop Mikha'il of Asyut, claiming that a first-century church was built at the location of the monastery in commemoration of the stay of the Holy Family, cannot be verified.[36] But in the Monastery of the Holy Virgin at Durunka, eight kilometers to the southwest of the city of Asyut, the belief is strong that the Holy Family had to travel farther south because Asyut (in those days, Lycopolis) was the nearest Nile port, and tradition (which was also recorded by Pope Theophilus) said they returned to the north by boat. "Where else could this have been but in Lycopolis?" Brother Luke, our guide in the monastery of Durunka, asks with a smile. "Here they found a cave near the port that offered them shelter until they could sail north."

Brother Luke firmly believes that there has been a church in the cave since shortly after the Holy Family's visit, although the first known record of the Monastery of the Holy Virgin probably dates from the beginning of the thirteenth century.[37] This tradition, Brother Luke says, has been confirmed by three recent appearances of the Holy Virgin. First, on January 22, 1980, she appeared to a deacon, then on January 10, 1988, she appeared in the church tower to an Australian woman, and Jesus appeared as a child

and as a dove to the workers of the monastery. Finally, on August 17, 1990, the Virgin appeared as a light in a room of the main cave.

The monastery has been completely renovated since 1955. The monastic complex today consists of many churches. The main one is in a huge cave that in pharaonic times probably served as a quarry. The Monastery of the Holy Virgin is better equipped than any other place on the route of the Holy Family to receive large numbers of pilgrims. For this purpose several hundred houses have been built against the slopes of the mountain, about one hundred meters above the agricultural land. From there one has a splendid view of the Nile Valley. At the foot of the Monastery of the Holy Virgin of Durunka lies a village, where the Catholic Church of the Holy Virgin receives pilgrims.

"In August we receive approximately fifty thousand pilgrims per day, and during the Great Procession for Virgin Mary on August 21, the number goes up to half a million in one day. During that day you can't see the floor—just heads of people," Brother Luke explains.

Pilgrims speak about an ecstatic experience when they describe their participation in the pilgrimage festival. In keeping with a long-standing tradition, Samir Naoum walked with other pilgrims along the road leading to the entrance of the monastery. He writes, "We followed the white-gowned deacons who processed in four lines, preceded by another group of deacons carrying a huge icon of the Virgin and child. Hymns were sung, and then the bishop appeared holding a large cross with which he blessed the gathering. Men clapped their hands, women ululated loudly, and four white birds were released as symbols of the Holy Virgin and of peace. This joyous occasion made a fitting culmination to my own flight into Egypt."[38]

Since the Monastery of Durunka started improving its facilities, it has surpassed the number of pilgrims going to the more historic pilgrimage site of Dayr al-Muharraq, which

The view of the Nile Valley from the Monastery of the Holy Virgin near Durunka. The church below is the Coptic Catholic Church of the Holy Virgin.

At this point on the west
bank of the Nile the
Holy Family may have
crossed to go to al-Qusayr
on the east bank.

today receives between two hundred thousand and three hundred thousand pilgrims per year. With this information in mind I asked Brother Luke, "Why do you get more pilgrims, even though the Monastery of al-Muharraq has such an important church and altar?"

Brother Luke at first evaded the question. "The difference is that Dayr al-Muharraq's pilgrimage season is during June and July, and the season for our monastery is from August 7 to August 21."

"But this doesn't explain the big difference in numbers," I pressed.

"Maybe it is because we have a bigger place than they have, maybe. Our bishop has arranged this place carefully. We have specific times for praying, for masses, for baptisms, for procession. In every place we have food, drink, water, toilets. This is a well organized place. It is more comfortable for people to visit—not like when you go to a place and feel very tired."

Both monasteries belong to the same church, and are only about fifty kilometers apart. They both have a link to the Holy Family, and they are both dedicated to Mary. They both try to attract many pilgrims. Could I call this 'a friendly competition'?

"Yes, yes," Brother Luke responded.

"Your monastery is named after the Virgin Mary, and so is the Monastery of the Holy Virgin of al-Muharraq and many other places. Why is this?" I asked. "Why don't you have a church named after the Holy Family?"

"That would be a Catholic name. We Orthodox won't dedicate churches to Jesus either. We have only churches named after saints. Because the Virgin Mary is the main saint, we dedicate many of our churches to her."

"Some Western scholars doubt the Holy Family actually stayed here. How would you respond to their scepticism?"

"We are Orthodox, and that means faith in tradition, certainly when the tradition is in accordance with the theological view. This is tradition that is not against mind."

Brother Luke brought us to a corner in the cave, which was blocked off by a door, but between the bars one could see a large modern icon of the Holy Virgin. "A few years ago the Holy Virgin appeared in this cave," Brother Luke explained. "We didn't see her face, but it was a miraculous appearance of light in the cave. We believe from traditional sources that this is the place where the Virgin Mary stayed. God confirmed our faith in this through a miracle. I am sure God wanted to tell us that this is a special place and a holy place. We only enter this cave during the procession in August, when our deacons carry this icon all around the monastery in the presence of our bishop or priests or monks."

Brother Luke continues, "You know, my name is Luke because I was a physician before I was ordained. You are asking about scientific evidence, but let me tell you that faith is more convenient to me than examining things on a scientific basis. Our Bishop told us once he was sure our Virgin Mary was here and is still here. This is the spiritual sensation, and we live by this sensation and not by logic."

Just as Father Philoxenos had done at Dayr al-Muharraq, Brother Luke made it very plain that Western arguments about the historicity of locations and manuscripts were not relevant to him. The development of a great monastery in a specific location means that that location had been blessed in the past, and if that is accompanied by miracles such as the appearance of Mary in Durunka, then God himself has given sufficient evidence that the Holy Family has been there.

Al-Qusayr

The return to Palestine through Lycopolis has become more and more accepted in recent decades, but there is also another, local, tradition according to which Joseph, after he was told by an angel to return to Palestine, took Jesus, Mary, and Salome to the nearest landing stage on the Nile, which was at al-Qusayr, only seven kilometers east of Dayr al-Muharraq. Those who believe that the Holy Family visited the cave near Durunka argue that the only main Nile ports in those days were at Lycopolis and Hermopolis (al-Ashmunayn). But Father Kyrillos of Sarakna says they could have taken a smaller vessel from al-Qusayr to al-Ashmunayn, from where they could board a larger boat.

Just as the Monastery of the Holy Virgin near Durunka is not mentioned in manuscripts about the flight to Egypt, so the church that became known as al-'Adhrâ' al-Rumaniya at al-Qusayr is not mentioned in any of these manuscripts. The tradition of al-Qusayr stems from the nineteenth century, when the Holy Virgin appeared in a cave near the Nile at al-Qusayr. Father Luka, whose great-great-grandfather discovered the cave-church, explained what his father and grandfather told him about this apparition: "Shepherds found the cave, and a woman in a shiny appearance appeared to them and told them to go out from this holy place, because they had taken their flock with them for shelter. We believe this woman was the Holy Virgin, and her appearance is for us an indication that the Holy Family visited this place. The shepherds told my great-great-grandfather the story and when he went there he found it was an old church, and he believed this must have been the same church old people in the area had been speaking about. He then assembled the heads of the main Muslim and Christian families in the area and they described the discovery." Father Luka produced the result: an old, yellowing document dated 1846, which he inherited from his father. "We believe Christians must have used this cave as a church during the Roman persecutions, and after the persecutions were over they went to the valley and the church was forgotten." Since its rediscovery, the church is used by the few Christians living on the isolated east bank of the Nile.

Local Christians doubt that the Holy Family would first travel fifty kilometers south from Dayr al-Muharraq and then return north. "Why

would they travel these extra kilometers if there was a landing place close by?" they ask. "Durunka is furthermore some ten kilometers west of the Nile, and boats could not even have reached there," believes Father Kyrillos of Sarakna. But Father Luka does not want to argue with the Monastery of the Holy Virgin near Durunka. "Whether they were in Durunka or not I don't know," he now says. "I only know for sure they were in al-Qusayr."

There is another tradition related to the area. Both Bishop Philippus and Fikri Ramzi report that some say that the Holy Family was not able to travel straight from Dayr al-Muharraq to Durunka "because there were difficulties," and thus "they went via Sarakna, Buq, al-Qusayr, and across from Dayrut, in a place known as the Cave of the Cow."[39] Father Kyrillos confirmed that Buq, a small town that was once a bishopric, five kilometers east of Dayr al-Muharraq, is on the road from Dayr al-Muharraq to al-Qusayr and according to a local tradition was visited by the Holy Family. When one crosses the Nile at Buq one arrives at al-Qusayr. "Local people also know of a 'Cave of the Cow,' which is about one kilometer north of the cave-church of al-'Adhrâ' al-Rumaniya, but no one relates it to the flight of the Holy Family," Father Kyrillos says. He believes it is more likely that the Holy Family visited Buq and al-Qusayr when they returned north. "Because al-Qusayr is so close to Dayr al-Muharraq, it seems logical that they took a boat north from al-Qusayr. Buq is on the route from Dayr al-Muharraq to al-Qusayr but it is more logical in my opinion that the Holy Family passed Sarakna before they arrived at Dayr al-Muharraq."[40]

A nineteenth-century manuscript describing the discovery of the Church of the Holy Virgin of the Romans inside a cave at al-Qusayr. The manuscript is signed by local Coptic notables who lived in the area at the time. The cave is connected to the Romans because it may have been used as a hiding place during the persecution of Christians in the third century.

The view from the east bank of the Nile at al-Qusayr. Inside the cave is the Church of the Holy Virgin of the Romans.

Traveling Farther North

According to tradition the Holy Family returned north via Hermopolis (al-Ashmunayn). Christians in Dayr al-Barsha, four kilometers south of Dayr Abu Hinnis, believe the Holy Family rested in the cave of the Holy Virgin in the mountains near their village on the east bank of the Nile. Meinardus reports that the cave is locked with an iron door and visitors need to ask the local priest to open it. "There is a painting on plaster showing the Holy Virgin seated on a chair and knitting. Moreover there is a carpenter's bench and plane, objects which according to tradition were used by St. Joseph." Meinardus also reports that pilgrims visited the cave, especially during the feast of Saint Bishoi on July 15.[41] Bishop Demetrius of Mallawi explained that this tradition has expired. "The key of the cave has already been in the hands of the Egyptian Antiquities Authority for several decades, and the tradition to visit the cave doesn't exist any more."[42]

Christians believe that the Holy Family arrived in Memphis, from where they then crossed the Nile to the eastern side, to what is now known as Ma'adi, where the Church of the Holy Virgin is found, and continued to Old Cairo, where they stayed again in the cave beneath the Church of Abu Sarga in Old Cairo.[43] From Old Cairo the Holy Family returned to Palestine overland, passing through On, Matariya, and Musturud. Meinardus mentions that they continued through Leontopolis, or Tell al-Yehudiya, to Bilbays.[44] Father Mina Ghabriel of Bilbays was not aware of this tradition. He knows Tell al-Yehudiya as a historical location, about ten kilometers outside Bilbays, but says there are no Christians living there. "If the Holy Family visited Tell al-Yehudiya, why doesn't it have a Christian church or community?" he asks. According to Meinardus, the Holy Family continued from Bilbays to Wadi Tumilat, which is equally unknown to priests in the area, and crossed into Sinai and went through Gaza to Nazareth as the angel had told them.

Bishop Philippus compares the return of the Holy Family to Palestine with Exodus 4:20, where God appears to Moses in a dream and tells him: "Go, return in Egypt: for all the men are dead who sought thy life. And so Moses took his wife and his sons, and set them upon an ass, and he returned to the land of Egypt."[45]

The entrance to the
Church of the Holy Virgin
of the Romans at
al-Qusayr.

What the Story of the Flight of the Holy Family means to the Egyptian Church

Fikri Ramzi refers in his book on the Holy Family to an article Pope Shenuda wrote in 1981, long before the preparations for the third millennium,[46] in which he stresses the spiritual value of the story of the flight to Egypt.

According to Pope Shenuda, God first called the people of Israel to him, and they were called "the people of God." But the prophecy of Isaiah 19 is the turning point because here for the first time Egypt—a nation of gentiles—was called to worship God, and God called the people of Egypt "My people," showing that God came not only for the people of Israel but for the entire world. Isaiah 19 is therefore a forerunner of the call in the New Testament for witnesses of God "to the ends of the earth" (Acts 1:8). In Mark 16:15, God says, "Go into all the world and preach the good news to all creation."

The second meaning of the prophecy of Isaiah 19, according to Pope Shenuda, is that God will come to Egypt, idols will be destroyed, and Egypt will know the Lord. The flight to Egypt is thus not just the escape from the evil King Herod, nor just a blessing for Egypt, but the beginning of God's message to Egypt: in all the places that the Holy Family visited, the faith in Jesus spread, which served as a preparation for the preaching of Saint Mark.

The story of the Holy Family, Pope Shenuda goes on to explain, is one of God turning evil into good: Herod's attempt to kill Jesus was turned into a blessing for Egypt, and over time, as idol worshipers rejected Jesus and the Holy Family was thrown out of a city, that city was punished, and the idol worshipers then understood that the power of God was greater than that of their gods. Furthermore, the story of the Holy Family shows that salvation was through the blood of Jesus Christ: Isaiah (19:19) prophesied an altar in the middle of a country of gentiles, which shows that Jesus is the real offering to the world. The offering foretold salvation through Jesus Christ: "For Christ, our Passover lamb, has been sacrificed" (1 Cor. 5:7).

Pope Shenuda believes that grace comes as an unexpected gift of God. The people of Egypt did not pray for Jesus to come, and they did not ask for his grace, yet this grace was offered to them. Evil should never be answered with evil. The Holy Family did not resist Herod's effort to kill them, but they escaped. The same happened to Jesus on the cross—he did not resist evil through fighting it but conquered it through his sacrifice. In the same way, martyrs did not resist evil but conquered it through perseverance in their faith, as Jesus commanded: "Do not resist an evil person" (Matt. 5:39).

Pope Shenuda concludes his explanation of the flight to Egypt by making it personal: "As Egypt opened its heart to Jesus and welcomed the Holy Family, so open your heart to God. What is the benefit if God comes for all Egypt, but does not come into your house?"

Conclusion

In many Egyptian publications the story of the flight to Egypt is presented as a static historical fact. Yet in the history of the church in Egypt, sites have appeared and others have disappeared. This is only natural, since the tradition depends on a living church, and Christians in Egypt very much want to be connected to the Holy Family's flight. This is why many locations can be found that are not listed in the official itinerary of the Coptic Orthodox Church but where local believers nevertheless claim that their churches have been blessed by the Holy Family. Also, new discoveries, such as the well at Tell Basta, the Floating Bible at Ma'adi, and the footprint of Jesus at Sakha, show that the tradition is developing.

Any site with a living church attracts large numbers of pilgrims, during *mulid*s and festivals, as well as at other times of the year. But at sites that no longer have living churches, such as at Farma, Tell Basta, Nikiou, Memphis, Dayr al-Muharraqa, and al-Ashmunayn, there is little to no pilgrimage, even when residents attempt to attract pilgrims. The tradition can only survive if there is a thriving church to carry it on.

Most stories told at the different sites concentrate on the struggle between the ancient pharaonic beliefs and the emerging church. The stories show how Biblical prophecies condemning the ancient beliefs were fulfilled. In these stories, Jesus triumphed over the idols, performed many miracles, and left signs of his majesty, such as the wells he created or the imprint of his hand or his foot in stone.

Miracles and the flourishing of sites such as the monasteries in Wadi al-Natrun and the historical churches in Old Cairo are often seen in retrospect as proof that the Holy Family must have blessed a location, and thus must have passed it. The standard reasoning is, how else could it be explained that a miracle took place at that spot, or that important monasteries and churches were built at specific locations and not somewhere else?

Most sites discovered to be holy in ancient times and sites that have only recently been deemed holy were revealed through dreams of saintly people, just as Joseph in the Old Testament and Joseph in the New Testament had revelations. Copts believe that the canon of the New Testament is not the end of God's revelations to us. They believe that revelations have continued through the ages to saintly people in the church who would not make statements if they were not

supported by known facts and tradition. Thus 'it is true if we have evidence,' which is a Western way of thinking, contrasts with the idea that 'it is true if it comes from a trusted source and it could be true.'

A monk at the Monastery of the Holy Virgin near Durunka.

Bishops, priests, and local believers tend to estimate the locations related to the Holy Family to be much older than archaeologists and historians do. Dayr al-Muharraq, for example, dates its church to the first century. Claims are often made that modern churches stand on the locations of very early churches that have disappeared.

Sometimes claims are made that the church is built over much older Jewish ruins, as at Ma'adi, or pharaonic remains, as at Musturud and Gabal al-Tayr. It seems that the farther back the history of a location goes, the more venerated the location.

The priests at Dayr al-Muharraq say the altar of the main church was consecrated by Jesus himself. No other church has as impressive a tradition, but many bishops and priests believe that churches were founded and consecrated by important saints. The priests at Dayr al-Muharraq say that their main church was consecrated by Pope Theophilus. It is also said that the venerable Helena, mother of Constantine, ordered the building of the churches of Dimyana, Daqadus, and Gabal al-Tayr. Christians in Dayr Abu Hinnis believe that their church was founded by Saint John the Short, who lived in Wadi al-Natrun but fled to the site of their village in 407 after raiders had made Wadi al-Natrun unsafe.

Last but not least, Copts believe the importance of the story of the Holy Family lies in its spiritual benefit for the believers of today.

Appendix
Annual Mulids and Spiritual Celebrations

Hundreds of *nahda*s are celebrated annually in the Coptic Orthodox Church, but only a few *mulid*s. This list contains all *mulid*s but only some of the larger *nahda*s at locations associated with the Holy Family, although most are not connected directly to the Holy Family. The date a *nahda* and/or *mulid* starts is flexible and can change. The *nahda*, however, always ends with a celebration on a fixed date.

In addition to the specific celebrations listed below, the traditional Christian holidays attract many pilgrims. Many people visit holy sites during the pre-Christmas fast, at Christmas and Epiphany, during Lent and Holy Week (with the exception of monasteries, which prefer not to receive visitors in Holy Week), and during the fast that precedes the Feast of the Apostles. Churches also attract pilgrims when they organize *nahda*s related to their patron saint. Estimates given below of numbers of pilgrims were obtained from local priests, who it must be remembered have no reliable means of making these estimates.

Baba 5–20 (October 15–30): *Nahda* at Dayr Abu Hinnis to commemorate Anba Yuhanna al-Qasir (John the Short), culminating in a celebration on October 30. During this period around five thousand pilgrims visit the site.

Baba 22–Hatur 7 (November 1–16): *Nahda* in commemoration of Mar Girgis in Dayr Abu Hinnis, attracting a few thousand worshipers.

Hatur 1–7 (November 10–16): *Nahda* in commemoration of Mar Girgis in the Church of the Holy Virgin at Harat Zuwayla, Cairo, with around a thousand worshipers each day.

Hatur 6 (November 15): Liturgy in remembrance of the consecration of the Church of the Holy Virgin at Dayr al-Muharraq by Pope Theophilus.

Hatur 28–Kiyahk 8 (December 7–17): *Nahda* dedicated to Saint Barbara at the Church of Saint Barbara in Old Cairo, attracting hundreds of worshipers.

Hatur 28–Kiyahk 3 (December 7–12): *Nahda* commemorating the medieval Saint Salib al-Gadid, the main celebration in the Church of the Holy Virgin at Harat Zuwayla, with over a thousand worshipers attending each day.

Tuba 3 (January 11 or 12): Liturgy in most churches in commemoration of the murder of the children of Bethlehem by Herod. At Dayr Abu Hinnis this is a large celebration with twenty to thirty thousand worshipers, and the bishop crosses the Nile in a decorated boat to lead a procession to Kom Maria.

Tuba 10–13 (January 17 or 18 to 20 or 21): *Nahda* of the martyrdom of Saint Dimyana at the Convent of Dimyana near Bilqas, culminating in a celebration of the day of her martyrdom on Tuba 13. This *nahda* attracts between ten and twenty thousand pilgrims. There are three liturgies per day, and an *'ashia,* or evening prayer, with a procession with an icon of Dimyana. Loudspeakers are used to allow people outside the church to hear the liturgy, spiritual songs, and messages.

Baramhat 3 (March 12): The Church of the Holy Virgin in Ma'adi embalms its relics in commemoration of the finding of the Floating Bible in the Nile in 1976, a festival attended by an estimated eight hundred believers.

Bashans 4–12 (May 12–20): *Nahda* and *mulid* dedicated to Saint Dimyana at the Convent of Dimyana near Bilqas, culminating on Bashans 12 in a memorial to the consecration of the Church of Dimyana. Some people arrive earlier, often as early as Shamm al-Nasim (the day after Coptic Easter). During the entire period, the *mulid* attracts, according to local estimates, perhaps one million pilgrims, most of whom stay in tents around the convent.

The ten days preceding Coptic Pentecost constitute Gabal al-Tayr's largest festival. Father Matta estimates that two million pilgrims visit the *mulid* during this period.

Bashans 23 (May 31): *'Ashia* in the Church of the Holy Virgin in Ma'adi, with around two thousand believers attending. Four or five hundred people attend the evening prayer in Sakha, commemorating the arrival of the Holy Family in Egypt: since the discovery of the footprint of Jesus in Sakha in 1984 the bishop takes the stone in procession through the church. Dayr Abu Hinnis celebrates this *'ashia* with a few hundred worshipers: the celebration includes a procession by the bishop of Mallawi through the church.

Bashans 24 (June 1): Commemoration of the Holy Family's entry into Egypt, celebrated in all churches, though the forms might differ. In Ma'adi and Sakha there is an *'ashia* on the previous evening, and in Ma'adi after the liturgy the following morning many people go out in feluccas on the Nile. In other churches, such as those at Samannud, Dimyana, Harat Zuwayla, Gabal al-Tayr, and Ishnin al-Nasara, this event is celebrated only in a liturgy on this day. In Musturud this date is the beginning of a *nahda*. At Dayr al-Garnus pilgrims attend a liturgy in the church: a cord is put in the well, as people believe the water rises on this day,[47] though they no longer check the cord to see how far it has become wet, as was done in medieval times. At Dayr Abu Hinnis some twenty to thirty thousand worshipers assemble on Kom Maria: the bishop crosses the Nile in a decorated boat and leads a procession to Kom Maria.

Bashans 24–30 (June 1–7): *Nahda* and *mulid* at the Catholic Church at Matariya commemorating the arrival of the Holy Family in Egypt. This *nahda* is preceded by the month dedicated to the veneration of the Holy Virgin. During this month and the *nahda* there are daily masses at 6:30 pm that attract between fifty and 150 people each day.

Bashans 24–Ba'una 8 (June 1–15): *Nahda* in the church of the Holy Virgin at Musturud celebrating the arrival of the Holy Family in Egypt, ending in the celebration on June 15 of the consecration of the Church of Musturud by Pope Mark III in 1185.

Bashans 27–Ba'una 4 (June 4–11): *Nahda* in preparation for the commemoration of Apa Hor in a liturgy on June 11 in the Church of Apa Hor at Sawada near Minya.

Ba'una 12–21 (June 19–28): *Nahda* at the Church of Harat Zuwayla in Cairo on the occasion of the Feast of the Theotokos, which attracts about a thousand worshipers each day.

Ba'una 14–21 (June 21–28): *Nahda* and *mulid* at the Monastery of the Virgin Mary at Dayr al-Muharraq and at Dayr Abu Hinnis leading up to the Feast of the Theotokos. The *mulid* at Dayr al-

Muharraq attracts anywhere from one to two hundred thousand pilgrims, most of whom come on the last day, which is the feast itself. The *mulid* at Dayr Abu Hinnis is much smaller and attracts between four and five thousand pilgrims.

Ba'una 21 (June 28): Feast of the Theotokos, Dissolver of the Iron Fetters. On this day many churches celebrate the release from prison in Philippi of the apostle Matthias (who had been chosen to replace Judas Iscariot; Acts 1:26) through the prayers of the Holy Virgin, the Theotokos, Mother of God. On this day the church also celebrates the dedication of the first church to the Holy Virgin in Philippi. Celebrations take place at Harat Zuwayla, the Monastery of the Virgin Mary at Dayr al-Muharraq, and Kom Maria, while at Dayr Abu Hinnis a procession is organized. At Gabal al-Tayr, the feast is celebrated only with a liturgy, while at Musturud and Sawada no liturgy is celebrated.

Abib 8 (July 15): Liturgy in remembrance of Saint Bishoi at the Monastery of Anba Bishoi in Wadi al-Natrun and all churches in the diocese of Mallawi. Bishop Demetrius of Mallawi hopes to turn the *mulid* at Dayr al-Barsha, which attracts some twenty to twenty-five thousand worshipers, into a *nahda*.

Abib 13–24 (July 20–31): *Nahda* and *mulid* of Apa Anub at the Church of Apa Anub in Sammanud, culminating in prayers throughout the night before the celebration on July 31. This event attracts a few thousand pilgrims, mostly families with sick children.

Misra 1–16 (August 7–22): The Feast of the Holy Virgin, commemorating her ascension to heaven. This is a period of fasting—no meat, milk, or other animal products are eaten. At most sites this feast is celebrated as a *nahda*. The Catholics, however, celebrate this feast on one day only, August 15. Most pilgrims visit the Orthodox *nahda*s and *mulid*s: The *nahda* in Sakha attracts perhaps one thousand pilgrims each day. The *nahda* of the Church of the Holy Virgin in Ma'adi attracts between a thousand

and fifteen hundred pilgrims per day, and perhaps five thousand on the last day. Old Cairo's largest *nahda* is at the Church of the Virgin Mary Qasriyat al-Rihan. The *nahda* at Dayr al-Garnus attracts a thousand to fifteen hundred pilgrims per day and develops into a *mulid* on August 21 and 22, with thirty to fifty thousand pilgrims. In the neighboring Ishnin al-Nasara the *nahda* attracts perhaps only three hundred people on the evening of August 21, because most people go to Dayr al-Garnus; on August 21 or August 22 the water in the well of Ishnin al-Nasara is said to rise at around 4 pm. At Dayr Abu Hinnis the *nahda* also turns into a *mulid* on the last days before the celebrations on August 21 and 22, attracting up to five thousand pilgrims. At Gabal al-Tayr, Musturud, and the Monastery of the Holy Virgin near Durunka, the churches organize *nahda*s but the celebrations develop into *mulid*s for most of this period. The largest numbers of pilgrims flock to these locations on August 22, when processions of icons of the Holy Virgin are organized. The *mulid*s attract many people who seek healing from evil spirits, and all kinds of diseases; others come to baptize their babies. Father Abd al-Masih of Musturud says most pilgrims visit the *nahda* and *mulid* at Musturud on Sundays, and he believes that up to one million pilgrims may visit the church on the first Sunday and up to a million and a half on the second. Brother Luke of the Monastery of the Holy Virgin near Durunka believes the *mulid* at his monastery can attract more than half a million pilgrims. The Catholics at Durunka have established a church at the foot of the monastery for their own pilgrims. The *mulid* at Gabal al-Tayr attracts more than a hundred thousand pilgrims. At most other locations many thousands of pilgrims can be seen. Also, places that no longer have a flourishing church, such as al-Bahnasa and al-Ashmunayn, attract pilgrims, but these are more for short visits than true pilgrimages.

Selected Bibliography

Abanub Louis, Father, *Hayat wa mu'gizat al-fata al-shahid Abanub al-Nahisi*, Bishopric of al-Mahalla al-Kubra, 1990.

Atiya, Aziz S., ed., *Coptic Encyclopedia*, New York: Macmillan, 1991. 8 volumes.

Coquin, René-Georges and Maurice Martin, "Dayr al-Muharraq," *Coptic Encyclopedia*, Aziz S. Atiya ed. New York: Macmillan, 1991a, 840.

———, "Dayr al-Muharraqah," *Coptic Encyclopedia*, Aziz S. Atiya ed. New York: Macmillan, 1991b, 841–42.

Demetrius, Bishop, *The Visit of the Holy Family to Mallawi*, 2nd rev. & exp. edn. Coptic Orthodox Diocese of Mallawi, 1999.

Fu'ad, Hala, "Hal sharib al-Masih min bi'r Tall Basta," in *Akher Sa'a*, May 31, 2000, 28–29.

Graf, Georg, *Geschichte der christlichen arabischen Literatur*. Biblioteca Apostolica Vaticana, vol. 1, 1944.

Gregorius, Bishop, *al-Dayr al-muharraq, tarikhuh wa wasfuh wa kull mushtamalatuh*, Cairo: [n.p.], 1969.

———, "Theotokos, Feasts of the," *Coptic Encyclopedia*, New York: Macmillan, 1991. *Kitab mayamir wa 'aja'ib al-'adhrâ'*, Cairo: 'Ayn Shams Press, 1927.

Ma'awad, Ibrahim Sabri, Father Rufa'il Sami, and Makari Armanius Surur, *Watha'iq tunshir li-awwal marra 'an rihlat al-'a'ila al-muqaddasa li-ard Misr*. Cairo: Mu'assasat Beter li-l-Tuba'a wa-l-Nashr, 2000.

Martin, Maurice, "Pilgrims and Travelers in Christian Egypt," *Coptic Encyclopedia*, Aziz S. Atiya ed. New York: Macmillan, 1991, pp. 1,975–77.

Meinardus, O.F.A., *The Holy Family in Egypt*, Cairo: Dar al-Maaref, 1986.

———, *Christian Egypt: Ancient and Modern*, Cairo: The American University in Cairo Press, 1977.

———, *Two Thousand Years of Coptic Christianity*, Cairo: The American University in Cairo Press, 1999.

Mingana, A., ed., "Vision of Theophilus, or the Book of the Flight of the Holy Family into Egypt," in *Woodbrooke Studies* 3.1, Cambridge: W. Heffner & Sons, 1931, pp.19–21.

Naoum, Samir, "An Escape into Egypt," *Al-Ahram Weekly*, January 7–13, 1999.

Nuns of the Monastery of Mar Girgis, *Rihlat al-'a'ila al-muqaddasa ila Misr wa mantaqat Misr al-Qadima*, Cairo: Dayr al-Shahid al-'Azim Mar Girgis, 1999.

Philippus, Bishop, *al-Sahaba al-muta'aliqa fi Daqadus*, Daqadus: Church of the Holy Virgin, 1994.

Ramzi, Fikri, *Alfan 'am 'ala magi' al-'a'ila al-muqaddasa ila ard Misr*, Published under the authority of metropolitan Athanasius, Cairo: Aghustinos li-l-Tuba'a, 1999.

Ramzi, Muhammad, *al-Qamus al-jiyughrafi li-l-bilad al-misriya*, Cairo: Dar al-Kutub al-Misriya, 1953–54.

Stewart, Randal, "Nikiou," *Coptic Encyclopedia*, Aziz S. Atiya ed. New York: Macmillan, 1991, pp. 1,793–94.

Tadrous, Ramzi, *Da'irat al-ma'arif al-qibtiya*, Cairo: self-published, no date.

'Umar, Mahmud, *Bi'r al-'a'ila al-muqaddasa*, Cairo: Madbuli, 2000.

Yacobus, Bishop, *'Adhra' al-Zaqaziq*, Zaqaziq: Coptic Orthodox Church of Zaqaziq, 1998.

Zaklama, Nashaat, *The Holy Family in Egypt* (English and Arabic), Cairo: self-published, 1999.

Notes

1   Meinardus, 1977, 619. The story comes from the vision attributed to Theophilus. See Mingana, 1931.
2   Bishop Yacobus, 1998, p.38.
3   *Ibid*.
4   Interview, February 2000.
5   Mahmud 'Umar published his findings in his book *Bi'r al-'a'ila al-muqaddasa* in 2000. Journalist Hala Fu'ad then reported the doubts of other archaeologists in the weekly magazine *Akher Sa'a*.
6   Interview, March 2000. Father Mina obtained his information from Bishop Gregorius's book on Dayr al-Muharraq (1969) and other church publications. The same story is mentioned by Meinardus (1977, 619–20). The text of Zacharias is published in *Kitab mayamir wa 'aja'ib al-'adhrâ'*, 70. See also the chapter of Stephen J. Davis in this volume.
7   Meinardus, 1977, 620.
8   *Kitab mayamir wa 'aja'ib al-'adhrâ'*, 71.
9   Meinardus, 1977, 621–22.
10 Meinardus, 1999, 20. Confirmed in an interview in March 2000.
11 Stewart, 1991.
12 Interview, September 2000. Geographer Muhammad Ramzi (1953–54, 464) believes the ruins of Nikiou are near Ibshadi, north of Zawyat Razin. Ramzi Tadrous (n.d., 75) places the location of Nikiou at Abyar, near Kafr al-Zayat.
13 Isaiah 19:18 calls the city the "City of Destruction."
14 Interview, September 1999.
15 Father Antonius of Ma'adi confirmed the existence of this oral tradition. The same story is also mentioned in Zaklama, 1999, 24.
16 Martin, 1991.
17 Bishop Philippus, 1994, 95. The translation of the Bible quoted here is the New International Version. The King James Version has "the princes of Noph are deceived" and "the children of Noph" respectively.
18 Coquin and Martin, 1991b.
19 Father Mikha'il al-Beheri (1848–1923) is a twentieth-century saint who was a disciple of Bishop Abraam of Fayoum. His death is commemorated on February 23, or Amshir 16.
20 Variations in spelling and transliteration are possible: Bisus and Bayt Bisus are also used.
21 While Father Shenuda believes that Cyriacus lived in the seventh century, this is not certain. See Stephen J. Davis, chapter 3.
22 Zaklama, 1999, 26–29.
23 Fikri Ramzi, 1999, 98.
24 Interview, March 2000.
25 Naoum, 1999.
26 Bishop Demetrius, 1999, 24.
27 On this day the apostle Matthias, who had been chosen to replace Judas Iscariot (Acts 1:26), was released from prison through the prayers of the Holy Virgin, the Theotokos ('Mother of God'). See Bishop Gregorius, 1991, 2,256. (He mistakenly says Ba'una 21 is July 28; the correct date is June 28.)
28 Mingana, 1931.
29 Bishop Gregorius, 1969, 75.
30 Interview, October 2000.
31 Interview, September 2000.
32 This number is probably related to the 144,000 who were sealed in Revelation

7:1–8. Father Philoxenos mentioned Yusi, as do most writers who cite the Arabic version of the Vision of Theophilus, *Kitab mayamir wa 'aja'ib al-'adhrâ'* (page 96). However, in the Syriac manuscript of the Vision edited by Mingana (1931), and used by Meinardus, Joseph's relative is named Moses.

33 Zaklama, 1999, 51. Zaklama took this quote from Bishop Gregorius (1969, 84). However, in Mingana's translation of the Vision of Theophilus, the text reads: "Any barren woman who beseeches me with a pure heart and remembers this house, I will give her sons" (1931, 36). The difference may be put down to the discrepancies between the Arabic text Gregorius used and the Syriac text Mingana used.

34 Coquin and Martin, 1991a.

35 Mingana, 1931, 37. Georg Graf (1944, 231) explains that the formulation "like a ship" refers to a "spiritual boat" that brought them back to Nazareth.

36 Meinardus, 1986, 59. This was also mentioned in the first edition of 1963.

37 Coquin and Martin, 1991, 799.

38 Naoum, 1999.

39 Bishop Philippus, 1994, 101; Fikri Ramzi, 1999, 133–34.

40 Interview, September 2000.

41 Meinardus, 1986, 62.

42 Interview, September 2000.

43 Meinardus (1986, 63–64) warns that medieval writers often transferred the name of Memphis to Misr al-Qadima, or Old Cairo, Local Christians today are unaware of this and mention Memphis and Old Cairo as two separate locations the Holy Family visited.

44 Meinardus, 1986, 66.

45 Bishop Philippus, 1994, 100.

46 Fikri Ramzi, 1999, 15–22. The reference is to an article by Pope Shenuda in *Watani*. May 31, 1981.

47 Meinardus, 1986, 42–43.

Visitors at the
Dayr al-Muharraq.

Ancient Sources for the Coptic Tradition

Stephen J. Davis

Introduction

In the Coptic Church, the traditions connected with the Holy Family's flight into Egypt occupy a special place in the hearts of the faithful. For centuries, the family's visit to Egypt has been celebrated in the Coptic liturgy. Churches and monasteries have been built over the sacred ground where Copts believe Jesus walked as a child long ago. Even today, pilgrims visit these sites in the hope of retracing his steps.

At the same time, the traditions related to the Holy Family in Egypt hold an interest for historians as well. One question that historians ask is, what are the sources for these traditions? For the historian, the written sources are important not simply as evidence for the 'itinerary' of the Holy Family—where they were thought to have traveled, and where not—but also as evidence for the beliefs and practices of the Egyptian church through the ages. What do the sources tell us about early beliefs concerning the flight of the Holy Family? What do they tell us about ancient and medieval practices connected with those beliefs? Ultimately, the act of exploring the writ-

ten sources is its own kind of historical pilgrimage. In the final part of this book, these sources will be our guide as we trace the development of traditions related to the Holy Family in Egypt.

The Original Story: the Gospel of Matthew

To find the earliest Christian source for the flight of the Holy Family into Egypt, one must go to the New Testament and the Gospel of Matthew. At the beginning of that Gospel, the writer gives a genealogy of Jesus (1:1–17) and an account of his birth in Bethlehem during the reign of King Herod (1:18—2:12). This account ends with a visit by wise men from the East seeking the birth of a king prophesied in the stars. The story of the Holy Family's flight into Egypt follows:

Now after [the wise men] had left, an angel of the Lord appeared to Joseph in a dream and said, "Get up, take the child and his mother, and flee to Egypt, and remain there until I tell you; for Herod is about to search for the child, to destroy him." Then Joseph got up, took the child and his mother by night, and went to Egypt, and remained there until the death of Herod. This was to fulfill what had been spoken by the Lord through the prophet, "Out of Egypt I have called my son." When Herod saw that he had been tricked by the wise men, he was infuriated, and he sent and killed all the children in and around Bethlehem who were two years or under, according to the time that he had learned from the wise men. Then was fulfilled what had been spoken through the prophet Jeremiah: "A voice was heard in Ramah, wailing and loud lamentation, Rachel weeping for her children; she refused to be consoled, because they are no more." When Herod died, an angel of the Lord suddenly appeared in a dream to Joseph in Egypt and said, "Get up, take the child and his mother, and go to the land of Israel, for those who were seeking the child's life are dead." Then Joseph got up, took the child and his mother, and went to the land of Israel (2:13–21).

Following this account, the gospel writer describes how the family settled "in a town called Nazareth, so that what had been spoken through the prophets might be fulfilled, He will be called a Nazarene" (2:23).

Two observations about Matthew's account are noteworthy. First, the story of the Holy Family's journey to Egypt is closely linked with the gospel writer's interpretation of Scripture. The flight and return is understood as the fulfillment of Old Testament prophecy. The key text for the writer is a quotation from Hosea 11:1, "Out of Egypt have I called my son." In Hosea, this verse was originally a reference to the Exodus, where Moses and the children of God were brought out of Egypt. In Matthew, the passage is interpreted in a new light: the gospel writer emphasizes Jesus' identity as the son of God, whose sojourn in Egypt fulfills biblical prophecy.

However, the writer does not want his readers to forget Hosea's original frame of reference, the Exodus. Throughout the Gospel of Matthew, Jesus is portrayed as a new, greater Moses. For example, Herod's 'massacre of the innocents' in Matthew 2:16 is reminiscent of Pharaoh's slaying of the Hebrew children in Exodus 2:15. Like Moses before him, Jesus survives a threat to his life in infancy and goes on to rescue his people.[1] The story of Moses is not the only subtext for the account of Jesus' exile in Egypt. Matthew's mention of Rachel weeping (2:18; quoting Jer. 31:15 [LXX 38:15]) also would have evoked for ancient readers the story in Genesis about her son Joseph's exile in Egypt, as well as God's call to her husband Jacob/Israel to go to Egypt after him: "I myself will go down with you to Egypt, and I will also bring you up again" (Gen. 46:4).[2] God's promise to Joseph's father in Genesis would have taken on new meaning for early Christians reading the story of the Holy Family's exile in Egypt and their eventual return.

A second element of Matthew's account, almost as important as its interpretation of the Old Testament, is its emphasis on geography. The second chapter of Matthew is dominated by geographical names: Bethlehem, Egypt, the land of Israel (the massacre at Bethlehem, Ramah), the bypassing of Judea, the resettling in Galilee, and Nazareth. The chapter carries the reader along on a virtual itinerary of geographical locales, an itinerary marked by biblical signposts. Indeed, each of Matthew's Old Testament quotations in this section feature geographical locales (2:15, 18, 23), and the initial reference— "Out of Egypt I have called my son"—highlights in advance the pivotal geographical movement of the narrative. In making Egypt the focal point of the story, the gospel writer draws richly on earlier biblical traditions in which the land of Egypt is both a place of exile and a place of refuge.[3]

In the history of the church, the Gospel of Matthew became the basis for later writings about the flight of the Holy Family into Egypt.

The two themes that I have highlighted—the interpretation of Scripture and a concern for geography—continued to play a key role in the development of later traditions surrounding the Holy Family. Later Christian writers diligently searched Scripture for other signs and prophecies of the family's flight. At the same time, writers also began to raise questions about where Joseph, Mary, and the child Jesus might have traveled while in Egypt, and what they did while they were there. Matthew's silence regarding their experiences and route of travel led to the rise of local traditions—first oral, and later written—about the wonders that Jesus performed in different Egyptian towns. From these traditions, the contemporary Coptic church has tried to reconstruct an 'itinerary' of the Holy Family in Egypt.

Biblical Interpretation and Controversy in the Early Tradition of the Holy Family

Hippolytus of Rome

One of the earliest post-biblical references to the flight of the Holy Family in Egypt may be found in the writings of Hippolytus of Rome, a prolific theologian and biblical commentator of the early third century. Hippolytus was also active as a church leader—during a period of disagreement in the church at Rome, he was appointed bishop by one of the opposing factions within the Roman community. In his *Commentary on Matthew*, he writes, "Concerning 'the days which will be cut short' (Matt. 24:22) because of the anger of the Antichrist—so the length of time of the Antichrist is three years and [six] months, for as long a time as Christ remained in his flight in Egypt."[4]

In the verse that Hippolytus quotes from the Gospel of Matthew, Jesus interprets a prophecy from Daniel concerning the end times, promising that God will "cut short" the sufferings of God's people in the final days. Hippolytus mentions the story of Jesus' flight in Egypt and interprets it symbolically as a sign for how long this "time of the Antichrist" would last—specifically, three and a half years. Hippolytus does not get this figure from Matthew. Where does it come from?

Again, the interpretation of Scripture plays an important role. In speaking about the "time of the Antichrist," Hippolytus probably had in mind the book of Revelation, where a period of three and a half years is twice mentioned in prophecies concerning the end times (11:2; 12:14). Like other early Christian interpreters of Scripture, Hippolytus was interested in numbers and their spiritual significance. This numerological interest helped shape his understanding of the Holy Family's flight.

Hippolytus may also have been aware of early local traditions about the length of the Holy Family's stay in Egypt. There are reasons to believe that the Roman writer had significant personal contact with the Egyptian Church. Hippolytus himself probably came from the East and perhaps from Egypt itself—in addition to a mastery of Greek language and philosophy, his writings also indicate training in the Alexandrian school of theology.[5] Hippolytus even seems to have spent some time with the celebrated Egyptian theologian Origen of Alexandria. We know that in the year 212, Origen came to Rome and attended one of Hippolytus' sermons. Through such connections, Hippolytus could have gained knowledge of early Egyptian traditions regarding the Holy Family. To this day in the Coptic Church, three and a half years remains the traditional duration of their time in Egypt.[6]

Origen of Alexandria's *Against Celsus*

The story of the Holy Family's flight in Egypt was also a source of controversy for early Christians in their debates with both pagans and Jews. In the second century, a Greek philosopher named Celsus actually accused Jesus of "having worked for hire in Egypt on account of his poverty, and having experimented there with some magical powers, in which the Egyptians take great pride."[7] Later Jewish writers would elaborate upon these accusations. A hostile tradition in the Babylonian Talmud (sixth or seventh century A.D.) claims that Jesus brought forth "witchcraft from Egypt by means of scratches [in the form of charms] upon his flesh" and that he "practised magic and led Israel astray."[8] The association of Egyptians with the magical arts was a pervasive cultural stereotype in antiquity, and accusations of magic were a common way of disparaging an opponent.[9] By means of such accusations, both Celsus and the later Talmudic writers tried to slander the character of Jesus and undermine Christian claims that he was the Messiah and son of God.

Such criticism drew lively responses from early Christian writers. Origen (ca. 185–253), the most influential early Christian thinker and head of the famous theological school in Alexandria, wrote the treatise *Against Celsus* in the early third century. It is an 'apologetic' work (from the Greek word *apologia*, meaning 'a defense'): in it Origen defends Christian teaching by highlighting points of disagreement with Celsus and debating his controversial claims. Commenting briefly on the subject of the Holy Family, Origen discusses the "miraculous circumstances" surrounding their "journey to Egypt." Whether the Alexandrian scholar had knowledge of any local traditions about Jesus' miracle-working in Egypt is unclear. By "miraculous circumstances" he seems simply to have in mind Joseph's angelic visions and the significance of the event in biblical prophecy.

Ultimately, however, Origen's main concern is not to provide an account of the Holy Family's journey, but to defend Christian doctrine concerning the identity of Jesus. Thus, he rejects Celsus' claim that Jesus' miracles were magical tricks learned in Egypt, and asserts that the flight into Egypt was simply further proof of Jesus' identity as the son of God.[10] The primary value of Origen as a source for our study is that he shows that the tradition of the Holy Family was known outside Christian circles as early as the second century.

Eusebius of Caesarea and the Interpretation of Isaiah 19

In the writings of Eusebius of Caesarea (Palestine, ca. 260–339) the flight of the Holy Family was the occasion for another controversy. This controversy was not related to an accusation of magic; rather, it involved opposing Jewish and Christian interpretations of biblical prophecy.

Shortly after 314, almost a century after Hippolytus and Origen, Eusebius wrote a work entitled *Proof of the Gospel*,[11] in which he discusses the flight of the Holy Family as a fulfillment of the Old Testament prophet Isaiah. Eusebius is best known as the author of the first *History of the Church*, but he also published a number of other writings. His *Proof of the Gospel* is (like Origen's *Against Celsus*) an apologetic work; in this case, however, Eusebius' purpose was to defend the Christian faith not against paganism, but against Jewish criticisms.

At two places in *Proof of the Gospel* (6.20 and 9.2), Eusebius comments on Isaiah 19:1 and interprets this verse as a prophecy of the Holy Family's exile in Egypt. "From Isaiah, an oracle concerning Egypt: Behold, the Lord is sitting on a light cloud and coming to Egypt; the idols of Egypt will be shaken by his presence, and their hearts will give way within themselves" (LXX).

The image of the Lord "sitting on a light cloud" caused difficulties for Eusebius in his debate with his Jewish opponents. Did Jesus actually come to

Egypt riding on a cloud? If not, could one still interpret this verse as a prophecy of Jesus' journey to Egypt? Eusebius' opponents raised these questions, and others as well: how could Christians claim that "the God above all gods" actually rode upon such a cloud and "walked locally on a particular part of the earth?" If Jesus did these things, how could he then still claim to be the infinite God (6.20.3–4)? Once again, the story of the Holy Family's flight into Egypt was a catalyst for controversy over the identity of Christ.

Eusebius' response was to interpret Isaiah allegorically. He argues that in fact there was no actual cloud that carried Jesus during the flight of the Holy Family. Instead, the cloud is meant to be a symbol of the divine conception of Jesus, of how the Word of God "took upon itself a body from the Virgin and the Holy Spirit" (6.20.6). Thus, for Eusebius, the Holy Family's visit to Egypt becomes a metaphor for the Incarnation, God's act of "becoming flesh" in Jesus Christ. By coming to Egypt as the Word made flesh, Jesus displayed a power that caused the idols and their demons to "recoil and be conquered" (6.20.11).

It is impossible to know whether this fascinating interpretation of Isaiah originated with Eusebius, or whether he was borrowing it from another source. If similar interpretations of Isaiah were circulating in Egypt in the early fourth century, Eusebius could very well have encountered them during his time there. Less than a decade before he wrote his *Proof of the Gospel*, Eusebius himself was forced to flee from Palestine to Upper Egypt (the Thebaid) to escape the persecutions of the Roman emperor Diocletian in 310.[12] In any case, the parallels between his own 'flight to Egypt' and that of the Christ Child may have helped spark his exegetical interest in the Holy Family.

The interpretation of Isaiah 19:1 as a prophecy of the Holy Family's flight has had a profound effect on later writers and the history of the tradition in Egypt. By the fifth century, writers had begun citing Isaiah to support local traditions about where the Holy Family traveled while in Egypt and about the wonders that Jesus performed in those places. In these local traditions, one finds the roots—the first traces—of what would later develop into a full-fledged pilgrimage itinerary of the Holy Family.

The Earliest Local Traditions: Ancient Hermopolis

In late antiquity, the city of Hermopolis (modern al-Ashmunayn) was a bustling metropolis on the western bank of the Nile. A district capital under pharaonic and Greek rule, the city hosted the main temple of the Egyptian god Thoth. During the Christian era, in the second half of the third century, the city became an episcopal see, and the temple of Thoth eventually fell into decline. This decline was accelerated by Christian settlement: archaeologists have discovered the remains of early churches built within the temple enclosure. Elsewhere in the city could be found a monastery dedicated to Saint Severus and at least seven other churches, including a large, three-aisled basilica from the first half of the fifth century. The granite columns and ornate Corinthian columns of this church, still in evidence today, indicate the wealth of the church in ancient Hermopolis.[13]

Hermopolis was also the first Egyptian city to be associated with the flight of the Holy Family: one Coptic scholar has called it the "place of origin" (*Ursprungsort*) for local traditions about the family's route of travel while in Egypt.[14] What are our earliest sources for these Holy Family traditions connected with Hermopolis, and what do they tell us about Christian beliefs and practices in that city?

Pilgrimage Sites Related to the Holy Family in Hermopolis

Around the year 400, an anonymous author wrote *A History of the Monks in Egypt*, one of our most valuable sources for the study of early Egyptian monasticism and pilgrimage. The *History of the Monks* describes the journey of seven pilgrims who traveled to Egypt from Palestine in order to visit holy persons and tour monastic sites in 394–95. The account of their journey begins in Upper Egypt at the city of Lycopolis (Asyut) and ends by the Mediterranean Sea at the mouth of the Nile. Along the way, the group stops in Hermopolis, and the author records their experience in that place: "We beheld also another holy man named Apollos in the Thebaid, within the limits of Hermopolis, to which the Savior along with Mary and Joseph came fulfilling the prophecy of Isaiah: 'Behold the Lord is sitting on a light cloud and is coming to Egypt. The idols of Egypt will be shaken by his presence and will fall on the ground.' For there we see the temple where, after the Savior had entered the city, all the idols fell on the ground upon their faces."[15]

It is clear from this account that, at the time of the pilgrims' visit, local traditions already connected Hermopolis with the flight of the Holy Family. As in the writing of Eusebius, the prophecy of Isaiah 19:1 plays a key role in this tradition. However, in the *History of the Monks*, Isaiah's prediction about the idols of Egypt is embellished slightly—in this reading of the text, the idols will not only "be shaken" but will also "fall on the ground." This extra detail was closely tied to oral traditions about the local archaeology. For residents and pilgrim visitors in late antiquity, the ruins of an ancient temple in Hermopolis were visible proof that the Holy Family had visited and that Isaiah's prophecy had been fulfilled. Could the temple in question have been the famous one dedicated to the god Thoth? If so, one of the churches constructed among the ruins of that temple would

The colossal columns of the basilica of Hermopolis (al-Ashmunayn).

undoubtedly have been dedicated to the Holy Family. Indeed, a twelfth-century catalog of *Churches and Monasteries of Egypt* mentions that in Hermopolis (by then called al-Ashmunayn) one could find "an ancient temple near the southern gate" containing several churches, including "a church called after the Lady, the Pure Virgin Mary" dedicated in honor of the Holy Family's visit.[16]

Another source for the Holy Family tradition in Hermopolis was a work composed by the Christian historian Sozomen in the middle of the fifth century (ca. 439–50). Originally from Palestine, Sozomen wrote his *History of the Church* in Constantinople and dedicated it to Emperor Theodosius II. This *History*, covering events during the years 325 to 425, provides more information about local sites associated with the Holy Family in Hermopolis.

In chapter five of this *History*, Sozomen records the following tradition about the Holy Family:

> At Hermopolis, in the Thebaid, is a tree called Persis of which the branches, the leaves, and the least portion of the bark are said to heal diseases, when touched by the sick; for it is related by the Egyptians that when Joseph fled with Christ and Mary, the holy mother of God, from the wrath of Herod, they went to Hermopolis; when entering at the gate, this largest tree, as if not enduring the advent of Christ, inclined to the ground and worshiped him. I relate precisely what I have heard from many sources concerning this tree.
>
> I think that this phenomenon was a sign of the presence of God in the city; or perhaps, as seems most probable, the tree, which had been worshiped by the inhabitants, after the pagan custom, was shaken, because the demon, who had been an object of worship, started up at sight of (Christ) . . . . It was moved of its own accord; for at the presence of Christ the idols of Egypt were shaken, even as Isaiah the

prophet had foretold. On the expulsion of the demon, the tree was permitted to remain as a monument of what had occurred, and was endued with the property of healing those who believed. The inhabitants of Egypt . . . testify to the truth of these events, which took place among themselves. [17]

Two observations may be made about Sozomen's recording of this tradition. First, his knowledge about the tree in Hermopolis is clearly based on oral accounts—at the end of the first paragraph he claims to write down "precisely what I have *heard* concerning this tree" (my emphasis). According to this oral tradition, a tree in Hermopolis was considered a place of healing for those who visited it and touched it, because this same tree had bowed low to worship Jesus when the Holy Family entered the city. Sozomen seems to have learned of this tradition from "inhabitants of Egypt." Second, Sozomen adds his own interpretation to what he has heard ("I think . . ."), connecting the tree again with Isaiah's prophecy concerning the "idols of Egypt." He surmises that the tree perhaps had once been the object of pagan worship, but that at the arrival of the Holy Family it had been freed of its demons. Sozomen here does not seem to be relying on earlier oral traditions about the tree; instead, he offers his own interpretation of the tradition. This interpretation may be his attempt to reconcile what he himself has heard about the tree in Hermopolis with Eusebius' earlier commentary on the Holy Family and Isaiah 19.

Sozomen's report about the tree in Hermopolis is most important for what it tells us about pilgrimage practice related to the Holy Family. In the fifth century, pilgrims visiting Hermopolis could witness not only ruined pagan temples as evidence of the Holy Family's visit (*History of the Monks in Egypt*, 8) but also an ancient tree whose limbs still bent down to the ground in honor of their passing.[18] Sozomen notes that the leaves, branches, and lower bark of this tree—perhaps the parts of the tree nearest to the ground where the Holy Family and later pilgrims would have walked—were thought to be specially invested with healing properties. His description is consistent with known practice at other early Christian healing shrines, where the act of healing was often effected by the touch of a sacred object. In late antiquity pilgrims often brought such objects home with them—clay flasks of holy oil, icons of the healing saint, amulets inscribed with a blessing and worn on a chain around the neck, even handfuls of earth or sand collected from a sacred site.[19] It would not be surprising if some pilgrims to ancient Hermopolis took leaves or sticks from this tree home with them as 'relics' of the Holy Family's visit.

The accounts in Sozomen and the *History of the Monks in Egypt* also reveal how the Holy Family traditions helped the church 'Christianize' the Egyptian landscape. In the tradition about the fallen pagan temple in the *History of the Monks*, one observes how ancient pharaonic sites could be connected with biblical stories and reclaimed as Christian sites. In the tradition about the tree, we see how natural features of the landscape were transformed into Christian monuments of the Holy Family's visit. Accounts of early Christian pilgrimage to the Holy Land give evidence of a similar process—in the minds of pilgrims, the Palestinian terrain often became imaginatively repopulated with the events and persons of biblical story. In this way, the landscape itself came to serve as tangible evidence for the stories told in Scripture.[20] In the earliest local traditions connected with the Holy Family in Egypt, one can see how Christians in the vicinity of Hermopolis had begun to re-envision their surrounding landscape as 'holy land.' For pilgrims in Egypt, as in Palestine, natural and historical features of the landscape came to be interpreted as markers of a biblical past.[21]

Later Sources: The Development of the Tradition

The tradition of the Holy Family's visit to Hermopolis is confirmed and developed in later ancient and medieval sources. The literary sources themselves are quite diverse: monastic biographies, Coptic martyrdom accounts, non-canonical gospels about Jesus' childhood, church histories, sermons, and other liturgical writings. What do they tell us about the development of the tradition in this region, and its spread to other locales?

First, these sources reflect early Christian writers' concerns about reaffirming the reliability and authority of the Holy Family tradition in Hermopolis. One way that writers did so was to identify famous Egyptian church leaders as authoritative sources for this tradition. Besa—biographer of the famous Egyptian monk Shenute (d. 466)—credits Shenoute with one such report about the Holy Family's visit to Hermopolis. In his *Life of Shenoute* (late fifth century), Besa describes how Christ appeared to Shenoute while the monk was traveling on a mountain in Upper Egypt. While experiencing this vision, Shenoute comes upon the unburied corpse of a man who had lived in the first century. Christ then raises the corpse, and the corpse tells Shenoute his life story. He recounts how he had heard about the Holy Family's visit while living in the city of Siut (modern Asyut): "The news had been spread abroad and came south to us by those passing through [the area] that a woman had entered the city of Shmoun [the Coptic name for ancient Hermopolis] with a little boy in her arms."[22] In late antiquity, reports about miraculous visions experienced by famous figures were commonly used by writers to bolster the authority of existing local traditions.[23]

Second, later sources also show how earlier stories connected with Hermopolis could be adapted, expanded, and even detached from their original setting. A prime example is the non-canonical Gospel of Pseudo-Matthew, one of a number of early Christian 'infancy gospels' that contain stories of Jesus' miraculous deeds as a child that are not included in the four canonical Gospels. In the Gospel of Pseudo-Matthew, the story of the fall of the idols in Hermopolis is embellished with new details. The author sets the story in a city near Hermopolis called Sotinen (otherwise unknown), and describes how a total of 365 idols were destroyed upon Jesus' entry into a local temple. He also appends a new episode about the reaction of the governor and priests in the city:

(22) And happy and rejoicing [the Holy Family] came to the region of Hermopolis, and entered an Egyptian city called Sotinen. And since there was in it no one they knew whom they could have asked for hospitality, they entered a temple which was called the "capitol of Egypt." In this temple stood 365 idols, to which on appointed days divine honour was paid in idolatrous rites. The Egyptians of this city entered the Capitol, in which the priests admonished them, to offer sacrifice on so many appointed days according to the honour of their deity.

(23) *But it came to pass that, when Mary entered the temple with the child, all the idols fell to the ground, so that they all lay on their faces completely overturned and shattered. Thus they openly showed that they were nothing. Then was fulfilled what was said through the prophet Isaiah: "Behold, the Lord shall come upon a swift cloud and shall enter into Egypt, and all [the idols] prepared by the hands of the Egyptians shall be removed before his face."*

(24) When this was told to Affrodosius, the governor of that city, he came to the temple with his whole army. And when the high priests of the temple saw that Affrodosius went to the temple with his whole army, they expected immediately to see his vengeance upon those because of whom the gods were destroyed. But when he entered the temple and saw all the idols lying prostrate on their faces, he went up to the blessed Mary, who was carrying the Lord in her bosom, and wor-

shiped him, and said to his whole army and to all his friends: "If he were not the God of our gods, our gods would not have fallen on their faces before him, and they would not lie stretched out in his presence. Thus they silently confess him as their Lord. And if we do not with prudence do all that we see our gods do, we shall perhaps be in danger of angering him and of all being destroyed, as happened to Pharaoh, king of the Egyptians, who was drowned in the sea with his whole army, because he did not believe such great wonders." Then all the people of the city believed in the Lord God through Jesus Christ. [24]

I quote the passage above at length because its structure is significant. One can easily distinguish how the writer brings the different layers of tradition together: he uses new legendary details (22 and 24) to supplement earlier local traditions (23, here in italics). Basically, he structures this passage like a sandwich. The original 'meat' of the tradition is the report about the fall of the idols as a fulfillment of Isaiah's prophecy (23); the newer traditions about the 365 idols and the governor Affrodosius are like fresh pieces of bread added to give the tradition more flavor.

Early traditions related to the Holy Family were not only expanded with the addition of new elements; they could also be detached from their original setting. As in the case of Sozomen's *History*, the Gospel of Pseudo-Matthew contains a story about a tree that bows down before Jesus and his mother.[25] However, the setting for the story is not Hermopolis; instead, the family's encounter with the tree occurs in an unspecified location in Egypt before the family reaches that city. The details of the story also differ significantly. In the Gospel account, the tree is a palm that bends down, not to worship Jesus, but to provide fruit for the Holy Family. The writer reports that at the command of Jesus, "the palm bent its head down to the feet of the blessed Mary, and they gathered from it fruits with which they all refreshed themselves." Also unlike the tree in Sozomen's account, the tree in the Gospel of Pseudo-Matthew does not remain bowed down, but receives permission from Jesus to raise itself up again. When it does, a spring gushes forth from its roots.

How does this account relate to Sozomen's original account about the tree named Persis in Hermopolis? It may, in fact, be a later version of the Persis story influenced by independent oral and written traditions about the Holy Family. One such tradition is recorded in the Quran. In Sura 19, when Mary is about to give birth to Jesus, she withdraws to a "far place" where she rests against "the trunk of the palm tree." There a voice, perhaps that of the newborn Jesus, cries out to her: "Grieve not! Thy Lord has placed a rivulet beneath thee. And shake the trunk of the palm tree toward thee, thou wilt cause ripe dates to fall upon thee. So eat and drink and be consoled . . ."[26] Is it possible that the story of the palm tree in the Gospel of Pseudo-Matthew was influenced by the Quran? Perhaps. In any case, it is clear that later Egyptians, both Muslim and Christian, connected these two traditions. The fifteenth-century Muslim historian al-Maqrizi, in his book on the *Topography and History of Egypt*, mentions (and refutes) a local legend claiming that Jesus was born under a palm tree in the Upper Egyptian town of Ahnas (modern-day Ihnasiyat al-Madina, twelve kilometers southwest of Beni Suef).[27]

The existence of folklore not initially attached to specific sites is significant for our understanding of how the Holy Family tradition spread and developed. Such independent oral traditions could easily be adopted later by other communities that recognized key features of the story in their local landscapes. In this way, any spring or fruit-bearing palm was, at least potentially, a site where the Holy Family may have rested. Today, at a number of sites connected with the flight to Egypt, sacred trees and holy springs are featured as local 'relics' of the Holy Family's visit.

The Spread of the Tradition in Upper and Lower Egypt

From Hermopolis (al-Ashmunayn) the Holy Family tradition eventually spread to other locales, probably first to other towns and villages of Upper Egypt, and later to areas in Lower Egypt (Cairo, northern Sinai, and the Delta). By the twelfth century, as more oral legends about the Holy Family were being written down and connected with other local landscapes, Coptic writers began to draw up quasi-official itineraries—lists of places where the family was thought to have stayed during their flight into Egypt. The sources for these legends and itineraries fall into four categories: homilies attributed to prominent Egyptian bishops; historical-geographical works on the church in Egypt; liturgical documents such as lists of saints' days and psalter readings; and infancy gospels. An examination of these sources can reveal much about pilgrimage related to the Holy Family in the medieval Coptic church.

It should be noted, however, that the study of the sources is a complicated science, full of hidden pitfalls for the casual historian. First, the date of the sources is often difficult to determine with precision. We either receive no information about their authors, or the works have been written pseudonymously—that is, under an assumed name, a common ancient practice by which works were attributed to esteemed writers from earlier centuries. Second, the itineraries presented often differ from one another, even when one compares different manuscripts of the same work. (See the appendix at the end of this book for a comparison of sources and itineraries.) One reason for such differences was the activity of later scribes who tried to 'update' older sources by adding new sites to their lists. Because of these factors, it is impossible to identify one universally agreed-upon itinerary in the medieval Coptic church. Instead, the itineraries themselves kept evolving as new local traditions were assimilated. Likewise, it is equally impossible to establish an exact chronology comparing the rise of local traditions at different sites.

Faced with such obstacles, how should an historian approach this evidence? For my part, I have decided to organize the rest of this chapter geographically, focusing on traditions related to some of the most prominent sites, specifically those places that are best attested in the sources. I will begin with sites in Upper Egypt, especially those in closest proximity to Hermopolis, where secondary traditions related to the Holy Family would have first taken root. Later, I will discuss selected sites in Lower Egypt, where the tradition of the Holy Family in Egypt gained a vitality of its own.

The Spread of the Tradition in Upper Egypt

The Town of Qusqam and Dayr al-Muharraq

The town of Qusqam (al-Qusiya)—located only thirty-six kilometers south of Hermopolis and fifty-three kilometers north of ancient Lycopolis (modern Asyut)—has a long Christian history. By 325 it was the seat of an early Christian bishopric. Later, the town and its nearby monastery, called Dayr al-Muharraq, would be among the first sites after Hermopolis to develop an extensive local tradition related to the Holy Family.[28] In medieval sources, Dayr al-Muharraq is recognized as the southernmost stop on the Holy Family's journey into Egypt.

The main source for this tradition is the *Vision of Theophilus*,[29] a homily attributed to the Alexandrian patriarch Theophilus of Alexandria that describes a vision of the Virgin Mary he experienced while staying as a guest at Dayr al-Muharraq. The work credits Theophilus' successor, Cyril of Alexandria, with recording the words of the homily.[30] In fact, given the style and content of the work, neither seems to have been the actual author. Instead, the writer was probably a later Coptic bishop who composed the sermon in the name of these renowned church figures. Such a sermon would have been first presented at Dayr al-Muharraq on a feast day dedicated to the Virgin Mary.[31]

The work begins with a celebration of this ancient monastery. Dayr al-Muharraq, located in the desert highlands outside Qusqam, is referred to as the "holy mountain" and is compared to the biblical sites of Mount Sinai and the Mount of Olives in Jerusalem. The writer understands Dayr al-Muharraq to be prophesied in Scripture. Indeed, the theme of the "holy mountain" appears often in Isaiah (11:9; 27:13; 56:7; 57:13; 65:11, 25; 66:20). The writer also quotes a prophecy from the Book of Revelation and interprets it allegorically as a further witness to the flight of the Holy Family:

I saw a woman clothed with the sun, and moon under her feet, and upon her head a crown of twelve stars. And I saw a serpent standing before her expecting her child that he might kill him, [a child] who rules the world with a rod of iron, and who went up to heaven unto God, and unto His holy throne . . . . I saw a dragon casting water out of his mouth after the woman that he might drown her in water. And the earth welcomed the woman, was rent and swallowed the water which the serpent had cast out of his mouth after her. And there were given unto the woman wings of a bird and she flew to the mountains, to a place prepared for her by God, and she inhabited it one thousand two hundred and three-score days, which makes three years five months and ten days [Rev. 12:1–6; 12:14–17, with changes].

In allegorical interpretation, persons and details mentioned in a text take on other spiritual meanings. Thus, for the writer, the woman in this passage stands for Mary. The sun in which she is clothed is Jesus Christ "who dwelt in her and illuminated all her body." The moon is John the Baptist "who was illuminated by the baptism of Christ." The crown of twelve stars symbolizes the holy apostles, who guide the church. The serpent is Satan, and the water from his mouth is "the anger which went out of Herod against the children whom he slew" after Christ's birth. Finally, the mountains to which the woman flees represent Egypt and the eventual site of Dayr al-Muharraq, where Mary and her child took refuge from Herod. (The length of their stay in Egypt is added by the writer, probably on the basis of local oral traditions.)[32]

After this introductory section of praise and biblical interpretation, the description of Theophilus' vision begins, in which Mary relates the history of her travels in Egypt, and especially her six-month stay in the vicinity of Qusqam. What can this account tell us about pilgrimage and religious beliefs connected with the Holy Family at Qusqam and Dayr al-Muharraq?

First, the writer of the *Vision* consciously links the traditions related to the Holy Family at Qusqam with those in Hermopolis/al-Ashmunayn. One way he does so is through the use of geographical 'markers.' The writer traces the Holy Family's route between the cities, describing how they traveled from al-Ashmunayn to Qusqam through a village named Qenis, and then later returned to al-Ashmunayn on their way back to Palestine. In this abbreviated itinerary, the time the family spends at Qusqam is bracketed (and highlighted) by their two stops in al-Ashmunayn.

Another way he links the sites is by 'recycling' older stories associated with al-Ashmunayn, and adapting them to the local context of Qusqam. In the *Vision*, the stories about the sacred tree and the fall of the idols at al-Ashmunayn are retold, and new legends are added. One such legend involves five camels that were turned to stone when Jesus passed by—a group of camel-shaped stones were apparently shown to medieval pilgrims visiting that city.

At the same time, the stories about the Holy Family's visit to Qusqam also highlight the fall of a pagan idol and a sacred tree. When the family arrives at the gate of the town, a statue with seven veils smashes on the ground after falling from the roof of a local temple. In response, the priests of the temple chase the family from the town with axes (this event leads Jesus to curse Qusqam and its inhabitants). Afterward, when the family stops for a rest outside the town, Jesus takes Joseph's staff made of olive wood and plants it in the ground, where it takes root. Jesus then blesses the tree "as perpetual memorial of my coming to this place."[33]

The borrowing and adaptation of such stories says something important about the relationship between neighboring shrines connected with the Holy Family. The promotion of these shrines would have fostered a curious spirit of both cooperation and competition among church leaders and pilgrims. Thus, in promoting Holy Family pilgrimage to Dayr al-Muharraq, the writer of the *Vision* honors the more ancient traditions at al-Ashmunayn, but at the same time presents new, rival versions of these traditions connected with Qusqam and its environs.[34]

In addition to the adaptation of older traditions, one also observes the development of new legends about the Holy Family at Qusqam. Sometimes these stories even introduce new characters—for example, the *Vision of Theophilus* includes Salome, Mary's cousin and nursemaid, as her companion throughout their travels in Egypt.

Another such story is the legend of the two thieves who encounter the family right after their entry into Egypt and pursue them all the way to Qusqam. While this story recycles elements of earlier legends (such as stories of a shady tree and a miraculous spring), its main purpose is to link the Holy Family tradition to the biblical narrative in a new way. When the thieves encounter the family in the highlands outside Qusqam, one of them (an Egyptian) has a change of heart while the other (a Syrian Jew) remains intent on stealing the family's garments. After blessing the repentant thief, the young Jesus then predicts that these thieves would be the two later crucified with him in Jerusalem:

[O Mary . . .] The Egyptian will be crucified on my right hand, and the Jew on my left, and the brigand who returned our garments will confess me and believe in me on the Cross, and will first enter Paradise before Adam and all his other children. You see also this spot where they have stripped me of my garments and you have shed your sweet tears over my body: all the sick persons who shall come to it in future and who shall be stripped on it of their garments and bathed in it, I shall heal them . . . . They will be made whole, and they will return home with joy and gladness. [35]

Here one sees how, in the *Vision of Theophilus*, independent legends such as that of the two thieves could be yoked not only with events narrated in Scripture (in this case, the Crucifixion) but also with local pilgrimage practices. A local healing spring near Dayr al-Muharraq—believed to have been formed from Mary's tears—later commemorated the Holy Family's encounter with the two thieves.

Other details about the family's stay on the "holy mountain" offer further clues as to what medieval pilgrims would have seen in their visits to Dayr al-Muharraq. According to the *Vision*, the small, abandoned house in which the family lodged became the foundation for the monastic church eventually built on the site. Local tradition holds that the original structure of the house was preserved in the church: before the family returned to Palestine, Jesus blesses it, saying, "As to this house nothing shall be demolished from it nor shall any thing be added to it." A well at the site that served the needs of the Holy Family became a place of healing. Indeed, the monastery as a whole gained the reputation as a place of blessing in the areas of work, health, and childbirth.

If the one who comes be a husbandman [farmer], I will bless his crops, and if he be a shepherd I will bless his flocks, and if he be a clerk I will bless his pen. If any of those who are versed in any craft come and pray in this house I will bless their craft. If any of those who are affected with a disease of any kind whatsoever come and pray in this holy house, I will heal all their bodies . . . And any barren woman who beseeches me with a pure heart and remembers this house, I will give her sons. [36]

The types of pilgrims mentioned here probably represent a cross-section of persons aided by the monks at Dayr al-Muharraq.

In the *Vision of Theophilus*, one also observes how Holy Family sites could be linked with the shrines of other saints. This is illustrated by the story of Joseph's relative Moses (in Arabic manuscripts, he is named Yusa and identified as Joseph's nephew).[37] After the Holy Family settles at Qusqam, Satan reveals their location to Herod, who then sends a group of soldiers to find and kill them. When Moses hears this news, he decides to go warn the Holy Family. Granted miraculous speed by God, he travels to Qusqam in only three days. Shortly thereafter, he dies in that place:

And [Moses] took the stone and placed it under his head, and turning his head toward the east he gave up the ghost. The old Joseph buried his body and interred it in this house under the threshold toward the interior. And his memory survives down to this day.

Buried in the wall of the church, the relics of Moses apparently became a secondary focus of veneration for medieval pilgrims visiting Dayr al-Muharraq. The pairing of saints and their shrines was a common feature of early Christian pilgrimage—such saints often came to be linked in local story and practice.[38]

Perhaps the most interesting new twist on the Holy Family tradition in the *Vision of Theophilus* is its account of a post-Resurrection visit by Jesus and Mary to the site of Dayr al-Muharraq.[39] In the *Vision*, Mary tells how Jesus appeared to her and the apostles in Jerusalem after his death and resurrection. After Mary recalls their journey to

Egypt, Jesus commands a cloud to come and carry the whole group (including Mary Magdalene and Salome) to the house where they had stayed outside Qusqam. There, Jesus and the twelve apostles consecrate the house as a church ("there was no church built in the world before it") and celebrate the first Mass. After having a feast, the group returns to Jerusalem on another cloud.

This account of a post-Resurrection visit to Qusqam shows once again how the prophecy of Isaiah 19 could be reinterpreted in a new local setting. Here, Isaiah's reference to a cloud is connected with a legend about the foundation of the church at Dayr al-Muharraq. In this way, the monastery and its church are implicitly presented as the fulfillment of Isaiah 19:19 ("On that day there will be an altar in the center of the land of Egypt"). Today, this foundation legend continues to play an important function at

Dayr al-Muharraq: for modern as well as medieval monks, the story represents a vital apostolic link between the flight of the Holy Family and contemporary monastic practice.[40]

Gabal al-Kaff (Gabal al-Tayr)

About forty-eight kilometers north of al-Ashmunayn, the Church of the Blessed Virgin Mary at Gabal al-Kaff ('mountain of the palm [-print]') perches atop a cliff that overlooks the Nile Valley from the east. The site, also known as Gabal al-Tayr ('mountain of the birds'), is recognized by most medieval itineraries as a place where the Holy Family stopped during their travels in Egypt. Among these itineraries, the *Churches and Monasteries of Egypt* (late twelfth / early thirteenth century) is our most valuable source because of the information it provides about local pilgrimage traditions.[41]

A view of Gabal al-Tayr in late afternoon light.

The old church at Gabal al-Kaff was hewn out of the mountainside itself. According to the *Churches and Monasteries of Egypt*, the name Gabal al-Kaff derives from a local tradition about a palm-print of Jesus preserved in the rock: when Jesus stopped at that place, the mountain bowed down in adoration of him, and Jesus restored it to its original position with his hand. For medieval Coptic pilgrims, the hand-print he left behind in the rock was an object of devotion.[42] It also seems to have been the source of a portable 'relic' that pilgrims could take with them from the church. Drops of a black substance named 'collyrium' could be extracted from a small fissure in the hand-print—perhaps this was one way that pilgrims could mark themselves as a reminder of their visit to the holy site.

In addition to this rock-hewn church dedicated to the Virgin Mary, the *Churches and Monasteries of Egypt*, attests the existence of a monastery at this location. The source also preserves a strange tradition that explains the alternative name for the site, Gabal al-Tayr. Apparently, on the festival day commemorating the death of the Virgin Mary, the site became known not only for the flocks of pilgrims, but also for flocks of birds that roosted in the nearby cliffside.

> At a certain place on this mountain there is a fissure; and on the day when that monastery keeps its festival, all the birds of the species called Abû Kîr come to this place; and it is a great wonder to see the multitude of the birds, and to hear their cries, and to behold their assembling around that fissure. Then, one after the other, without ceasing, they insert their heads into the fissure, and place their beaks into the cavity of the mountain, and utter a cry and come away; and this they do until the head of one of them is caught in the fissure, and he hangs there, beating his wings until he dies; and after that all the birds fly away until not one of them is left there.[43]

Today, while birds no longer congregate at Gabal al-Kaff, both Coptic and Muslim pilgrims still come in large numbers to celebrate the Holy Family's visit.

Paisus near al-Bahnasa
Another Upper Egyptian site connected with the Holy Family in medieval itineraries was a monastery called Paisus, now Dayr al-Garnus, located near the town of Ishnin al-Nasara, about ten kilometers northeast of al-Bahnasa (ancient Oxyrhynchus). The sources actually contain several variations on the place name. 'Paisus' probably derives from the Coptic *pa-Isous*, meaning '(a place) belonging to Jesus.' The site is also referred to as *Bisus* ('[a place named] after Jesus'), *Bayt Isus* ('house of Jesus'), and *Dayr Isus* ('monastery of Jesus'). While Paisus is cited as early as the twelfth century, the sources in this period give little information about the site itself. [44] For example, Abu al-Makarim seems to have been confused over the exact location of the monastery, and only mentions that the monastery had a well that rose and fell with the Nile tide.[45]

One of our main sources of information for al-Bahnasa and this 'Monastery of Jesus' is a homily attributed to Cyriacus, a bishop of al-Bahnasa.[46] Although he is credited with other works, we have no historical information about Cyriacus himself. Estimates of his dates have ranged widely, from the sixth to the fifteenth century.[47]

The homily of Cyriacus relies in part on the *Vision of Theophilus* and shares with it common motifs designed to bolster the authority of the tradition being presented. Two of these motifs are the appeal to heavenly vision and the tracing of local tradition directly to a member of the Holy Family (Joseph). Cyriacus describes how, through divine revelation, a local priest named Antonius discovers a treasure and an ancient document hidden in an ancient church. The ancient document that he finds is supposed to have been written by a fourth-century priest named Thomas—in the document, Thomas reports about his own miraculous discovery of a book written by Joseph himself. Thus, through an elaborate 'genealogy' of visions and discoveries, the homily seeks to trace its authority back to the words of an actual eyewitness. In this way, the 'book of Joseph' functions as a written counterpart to Mary's revelation in the *Vision of Theophilus*.[48]

In contrast to the *Vision*, though, the Holy Family traditions preserved in Cyriacus' sermon are closely, indeed almost exclusively, tied to the monastery named Paisus and the area around al-Bahnasa. Despite this fact, the sermon clearly relies on earlier traditions from other locales. For example, when the family arrives at al-Bahnasa, they are greeted by a fall of the idols, just as in al-Ashmunayn: "(The idols) immediately fell upon the ground and broke, and their attendants ran away." Later, at Paisus, Joseph plants a staff into the ground and it instantly blooms and grows into a tree; the tree then bows down low to the ground in homage to the Christ Child (here we have a mingling of stories from both al-Ashmunayn and Qusqam).[49]

About the setting of Paisus itself we learn little from Cyriacus. The monastery seems to have been situated in an agricultural area—much of the account about the Holy Family's visit involves their hospitable reception by a local farmer who brings them back to his home (the site of the future monastery). While there, the farmer takes Jesus out to bless his sheep. As in the case of other Holy Family sites, the monastery gained the reputation as a place of healing for visitors: "the blind saw, the deaf heard, the lepers were cleansed, the mute talked, by the power of God."[50] Finally, Cyriacus also hints at the practice of local saint veneration at the monastery: after the farmer dies, he is said to have been buried within "that holy place." As a sacred site of healing and saint veneration, the Monastery of Jesus would have attracted both Christian and Muslim pilgrims during the medieval period.[51]

The Spread of the Tradition in Lower Egypt and Northern Sinai

Medieval sources also attest to a number of places in Lower Egypt linked with Holy Family devotion. In fact, the pattern of devotion and pilgrimage in the north had its own unique character. Even more than in the south (where traditions largely sprang from a single point of origin and spread to other locations along the Nile), the proliferation of sites in Lower Egypt was closely linked with a concern for tracing the exact footsteps of the Holy Family. Early on, knowledge of the early Holy Family tradition at al-Ashmunayn would have led the churches of Lower Egypt and the northern Sinai to ask, where did Jesus pass on his way southward? Later, with the rise of different local traditions in the north, church writers began to gather these sites into coherent (and sometimes not so coherent) accounts of the family's route of travel.

As in Upper Egypt, the dating of such traditions is often difficult to determine. However, at least in a couple of locations, there are indications that Holy Family traditions may have arisen even earlier than at Upper Egyptian sites such as Dayr al-Muharraq and Gabal al-Kaff. While the formal itineraries date to the twelfth century and later, a few isolated local traditions appear even earlier in the travel diaries of late antique pilgrims.

One such diary was written by an anonymous pilgrim from Piacenza, Italy, in the late sixth century.[52] It is the earliest source documenting Holy Family traditions in Lower Egypt; indeed, no other available source for this region can be definitively dated earlier than the ninth century. In this diary, the pilgrim recounts a visit he made to the city of Memphis, located just southwest of Cairo. There he claims to have seen an ancient temple whose door had been miraculously sealed shut at the arrival of the Holy Family—the temple was later converted into a church. At the same site, he also saw "a linen cloth, upon which was a portrait of the Saviour, who, as the people said, wiped his face upon it, and his image remained there."[53] Apparently, this cloth was brought out on special occasions for veneration by worshipers and visitors. Unfortunately, these early traditions recorded by the Piacenza pilgrim appear in no other sources, and they may subsequently have been lost or forgotten.

In most places, however, local traditions about the Holy Family seem to have endured, largely because of their inclusion in 'official' medieval itineraries. My discussion of sites and sources below generally follows the path of these itineraries, starting first with northern Sinai, then the Delta, and finally the city of Cairo.

Farama

The city of Farama (ancient Pelusium) is located near the Mediterranean coast in northern Sinai. An active seaport in antiquity, it became known in early Christian history as a center of monasticism.[54] By the ninth century, the city of Farama was also celebrated as a stopping point for the Holy Family on their journey across Sinai. While not always included in the Coptic-Arabic itineraries, it is mentioned in ninth-century accounts by the Greek monk Epiphanius and Bernard the Wise, a pilgrim to the Holy Land (ca. 870). Bernard tells how he stopped at Farama, where he saw "a church of Saint Mary, on the spot to which by the admonition of the angel, Joseph fled with the child and its mother." He then adds, "In this city, there is a multitude of camels, which are hired for the natives by the travellers to carry their baggage across the desert [to Jerusalem], which is a journey of six days." Bernard provides no more details about the church, but his account does show how an Egyptian site connected to the Holy Family could be incorporated into the 'tourist package' for pilgrims traveling to and from the Holy Land.[55]

Tell Basta

Most of the medieval Arabic sources recognize Tell Basta, a town in the eastern Delta, as the Holy Family's first stop in Egypt proper. There,

according to the *Vision of Theophilus*, the inhabitants of the town refused to welcome them or supply them with water. In the *Vision*, Tell Basta is also identified as the place where the Holy Family first encountered the two robbers on their way into Egypt. After the robbers steal Jesus' sandals, Mary starts weeping in the shade of a large tree. To comfort her, Jesus wipes off her tears and makes the sign of the cross on the ground. At that spot, a spring immediately wells up and the family satisfies their thirst. Here again, a story about the Holy Family is designed to explain the existence of a spring (and a tree) blessed by Christ for the healing of pilgrims and visitors.[56]

In the later Ethiopian *Narrative of the Virgin Mary*, another tradition about Mary's visit to Tell Basta suggests an interesting interplay between Holy Family written legends and later iconography.[57] After the local citizens refuse to welcome the Holy Family, Joseph becomes tired because of the heat: "Behold, I am toiling in a manner that is above my strength, and I cannot [go on] doing so because of my old age." When Mary sees his struggles, she asks the infant Jesus why they must suffer so much for his sake. In response, Jesus stops sucking from her breast and tells his tired father to carry him "in order that I may lay my hand upon thy breast so that thy soul may become strong." Obeying, Joseph lifts Jesus up and puts him "upon his shoulder," and as soon as Jesus lays his hand upon his breast, Joseph's fatigue vanishes. What is interesting about this story is its relationship to Coptic iconography of the Holy Family. The image of Joseph carrying Jesus on his shoulder is a popular one in nineteenth- and twentieth-century Coptic icons.[58] This image may have originally been based on this scene from the *Narrative of the Virgin Mary*.

Bikha Isous and the Towns of the Central Delta

The towns of the central Delta are unfortunately not well referenced in the earliest sources. One of the best-attested traditions concerns a place called

Bikha Isous ('foot of Jesus'), which is mentioned by both Abu al-Makarim and the Arabic Synaxarium (a liturgical calendar of Coptic saints and their festivals).[59] The Synaxarium locates Bikha Isous west of the village of Samannud, and tells the story of how Jesus "pressed his heel into a stone" as a sign of his visit to that place. Abu al-Makarim's *Churches and Monasteries of Egypt* provides more details about this local tradition. According to his account, Bikha Isous was the name of a monastery built on the site of a Roman bath at Minyat Tana (as a result, the monastery also went by the name Dayr al-Maghtis, or 'monastery of the bath'). After telling the story of Jesus' footprint in more detail, Abu al-Makarim describes how the stone became an object of devotion for later pilgrims. Some pious visitors would put oil on the stone and carry it around the area. By the time of his writing, however, this relic had become lost. The monks, fearing that pilgrims would do damage to the stone, decided to hide it in a secret place: "No one knows the location up to the present day." Eventually, along with this stone, the original location of Bikha Isous was also forgotten. Today, the church at Sakha claims to be the lost site of Bikha Isous. This local claim arose fifteen years ago with the discovery of a stone with a child's footprint outside the church walls.[60]

Later sources fill in the route of the Holy Family between Tell Basta and Bikha Isous. Perhaps our most important source is a homily attributed to Zacharias, bishop of Sakha, a Delta town located northwest of Samannud. Zacharias, who lived during the late seventh and early eighth centuries, was a monk in Wadi al-Natrun before being ordained bishop.[61] He was also a prolific writer. However, again, it is doubtful that Zacharias himself wrote this homily in its present form; it is more likely that a later bishop of Sakha wrote (or revised) the work in Zacharias' name in order to promote Holy Family devotion in the Delta and in the monasteries of Wadi al-Natrun.[62]

The *Homily of Zacharias* borrows substantially from the earlier *Vision of Theophilus*, but also adds its own material. A simple comparison between the *Vision of Theophilus* and this homily of Zacharias shows how the itinerary of the Holy Family was expanded in this work to include sites in the Delta.[63]

Vision of Theophilus	Homily of Zacharias
Tell Basta	Tell Basta
	Minyat Ganah (= Minyat Samannud)
	Burulus
	Shagarat al-Tin al-[M]atla'
	Bikha Isous (= Dayr al-Maghtis) (= Minyat Tana)
	Gabal al-Natrun
al-Ashmunayn	al-Ashmunayn
Qusqam (= Dayr al-Muharraq)	Dayr al-Muharraq

In comparing the two lists, one readily observes the series of locations added in the later work (from Minyat Ganah to Gabal al-Natrun). Later editions of the *Homily* expand the list of Delta sites even farther to include places such as al-Mahamma, Bilbays, and Bilad al-Sibakh.[64]

It is interesting that the connection between the Delta and Wadi al-Natrun in Zacharias' life is also reflected in this itinerary of the Holy Family. In the *Homily of Zacharias*, after the family visits the Delta, they proceed directly to Wadi al-Natrun (Gabal al-Natrun); there Jesus gazes over the area and predicts that it would become a special abode for monks. The inclusion of Gabal al-Natrun in the itinerary may reflect the writer's desire to honor the memory of Zacharias, who spent part of his life there as a monk at the Monastery of Saint John the Short.

Matariya and Old Cairo

Holy family traditions in and around Cairo are better documented than those in the Delta, although their placement in the medieval itineraries varies. In most sources, the family stops at Matariya and Old Cairo on their way south toward Upper Egypt. However, in two liturgical texts—the Arabic Synaxarium and the *Difnar* (a collection of hymns used in the Coptic Church)—the order is reversed: the family visits Cairo as they travel north on their way back to Palestine.

Matariya, a district about ten kilometers northeast of downtown Cairo, is another place where local tradition about Jesus' visit involves a sacred tree and sacred spring. The Arabic Infancy Gospel reports that the Holy Family came to a "sycamore tree which is today called Matariya." This tree is said to have grown from a spot where Jesus' sweat dropped upon the ground. At that same place, Jesus causes a spring to gush forth from the ground, and Mary washed her clothes in the water. The Arabic Synaxarium claims that Mary actually bathed in this spring, and as a result, the water of the spring became sanctified—oil from the tree mixed with water from the spring was used in baptism and in the consecration of churches. In the Arabic and Ethiopian Synaxaria, the tree at Matariya is not a sycamore, but a balsam. The Ethiopian Synaxarium even gives a different explanation for the origin of the tree, a variation on earlier legends about Joseph's staff. In this source, Jesus takes the staff from his father, breaks it into pieces, and plants them in the ground. After he waters the spot with water from the spring, the staff sprouts into a tree.[65]

The famous tree at Matariya was visited by a stream of international pilgrims in the Middle Ages, many of whom were on their way to or from the Holy Land.[66] Their personal testimony reveals much about local pilgrimage practices and the rise of secondary legends at the site. The pilgrim Burchard of Mount Sion (1285–95) describes how he bathed in the spring in the belief that Mary had dipped Jesus in the water. Before he departed, he gathered wood from the tree as a holy souvenir. This practice of 'pious pruning' was apparently curbed somewhat in later centuries (perhaps because the tree began looking a bit too bare). In the fifteenth century (1435–39), a pilgrim named Pero Tafur reports that no one who entered the site was allowed to clip off leaves or twigs from the tree.[67]

Legends also grew up around other trees at Matariya, just as new legends were told about the main tree at the site. In the fourteenth century, the pilgrim Marino Sanuto (1321)[68] claims to have seen a sacred palm tree at the site—the very one that had inclined its branches so that Mary could gather its fruit. According to Sanuto, some pagans cut the tree down at one point, but it raised itself up again overnight. He probably gained this knowledge about the tree from one of the guardians at the site, because as evidence for the story he was shown the knife marks that were supposedly still visible in the wood.[69] Another pilgrim, a Dominican monk named Felix Fabri, visited Matariya in the fifteenth century (1480).[70] There he claims to have seen a fig tree with a hollow trunk near the gate of the enclosure. According to local tradition at that time, the tree had opened up to provide refuge for the Virgin Mary, and two lamps hung inside the tree to commemorate this event. Fabri also gives a different explanation for the origin of the balsam tree at Matariya. According to him, the balsam was originally a gift from the Queen of Sheba to King Solomon; it was later transplanted to Egypt by Caesar Augustus, but it did not flourish until the arrival of the Holy Family. Here again, we see how, for pilgrims like Fabri, such local legends effectively linked the landscape at Matariya more closely to events from the biblical past.

The traditions connected with the Holy Family at Old Cairo may be even older than those at Matariya. The literary sources identify several churches in Old Cairo as places where the Holy Family was thought to have visited. However, these sources reveal little about local legends or the practice of pilgrimage at these churches.

Of all the sites in Old Cairo, the Church of Abu Sarga (Saint Sergius) is best attested: it is mentioned in several liturgical texts, including the Arabic Synaxarium and the *Difnar*. These sources tell how the Holy Family, on arrival in Old Cairo (ancient Babylon), took refuge in a cave, located "in the church of Abu Sarga."[71] This cave may still be seen by those visiting the church today.

In addition to Abu Sarga, one finds references to other sites in and around Old Cairo. The *History of the Patriarchs in the Egyptian Church* (twelfth century) mentions the nearby al-Mu'allaqa Church ('the hanging church') in its list of places where the Holy Family stayed during their flight in Egypt. The church takes its name from the fact that it was built over the Roman fortress of Babylon in Old Cairo. One section of the church juts out over the empty interior of one of the fortress towers. The *History of the Patriarchs* also names a Church 'At the Steps' in Cairo—today, the Church of the Virgin Mary at Ma'adi (a suburb twelve kilometers south of Old Cairo) features a flight of steps leading down to the Nile. From these steps Jesus, Mary, and Joseph are supposed to have embarked on their journey to Upper Egypt.

Finally, the *Churches and Monasteries of Egypt* mentions a Church of al-Martuti located south of Old Cairo near a garden called al-'Adawiya.[72] The actual location of this site is somewhat uncertain. The village of al-'Adawiya lies about twenty-nine kilometers south of Old Cairo; but if the Church of al-Martuti was at one time found there, it no longer exists. Today, the Church of the Virgin Mary at Ma'adi mentioned above claims that it occupies the site of this medieval Church of al-Martuti.[73]

According to Abu al-Makarim, the church's name reflected the fact that it was dedicated to the Virgin Mary—'al-Martuti' is said to derive from the Greek words meaning 'mother of God' (*mêtêr theou*). Indeed, as in many contemporary Coptic churches, an icon of the Virgin was displayed before the altar of the thirteenth-century church.

But what is most interesting about Abu al-Makarim's report is the fact that he links this church not only with the flight of the Holy Family, but also with the earlier exile of the Israelites in the Old Testament:

> In ancient days this was a place of worship of the Israelites when they were in bondage in Egypt; and when our Lord Jesus Christ came down into Egypt from Syria, with his mother in the flesh, our Lady the Pure Virgin, and the righteous old man Joseph the carpenter, they sat in this place, where there is now a picture of the Lady before the holy altar.[74]

This local tradition underscores once again the importance of biblical interpretation in the promotion of Holy Family sites. By connecting the Church of al-Martuti with multiple layers of biblical history, the writer presents the church as part of a rich biblical landscape—a landscape that pilgrims themselves could imaginatively enter. In this way, pilgrims worshiping in the church and gazing at the icon of the Virgin could truly envision themselves standing in the footsteps both of the Holy Family and of the ancient people of God.

Conclusion

In the latter part of this chapter, I have focused my attention on the sites best attested in the ancient and medieval sources. An examination of the itinerary charts in the appendix of this book will show how the list of sites associated with the Holy Family continued to be expanded in the late medieval and early modern periods as new local traditions asserted themselves and as earlier works were revised to accommodate these new traditions. The rise of these new traditions was again motivated by familiar factors: the interpretation of Scripture in new contexts, the authority of divine visions, the miraculous discovery of new artifacts, the desire to fill 'gaps' in the route of the Holy Family. These factors have shaped the perceptions of Coptic pilgrims throughout the centuries, and indeed these same factors still mark the vitality of Holy Family devotion today.

Appendix
A Comparison of Select Sources and Sites

Table 1: Homilies attributed to Theophilus of Alexandria and Zacharias of Sakha

TS	TA1	TA2	Z	Z1
Tell Basta	Tell Basta	Tell Basta	Tell Basta	Tell Basta
	al-Mahamma	al-Mahamma		al-Mahamma
		Bilbays		Bilbays
		Minyat Ganah	Minyat Ganah	Minyat Ganah
		Samannud	Samannud	Samannud
		Burulus	Burulus	Burulus
			Shagarat al-Tin	Shagarat al-Tin
		al-Matla'	al-[M]atla'	al-Matla'
		Bilad al-Sibakh		Bilad al-Sibakh
			Bikha Isous (= Dayr al-Maghtis) (= Tana)	Bikha Isous (= Dayr al-Maghtis)
		Gabal al-Natrun	Gabal al-Natrun	Gabal al-Natrun
		'Ayn Shams (= Matariya)		Matariya (= 'Ayn Shams)
		Old Cairo (= Abu Sarga)		Old Cairo (= Abu Sarga)
	Gabal al-Kaff			Gabal al-Kaff
al-Ashmunayn	al-Ashmunayn	al-Ashmunayn	al-Ashmunayn	al-Ashmunayn
Qusqam (= Dayr al-Muharraq)	Qusqam (= Dayr al-Muharraq)	Qusqam (= Dayr al-Muharraq)	Qusqam (= Dayr al-Muharraq)	Qusqam (= Dayr al-Muharraq)

TS = *Vision of Theophilus* (Syriac).
A. Mingana, ed. "Vision of Theophilus, or the Book of the Flight of the Holy Family into Egypt," *Woodbrooke Studies* 3.1 (Cambridge: W. Heffer & Sons, Ltd., 1931), 1–43 (English translation), 44–92 (Syriac text).

TA1 = *Vision (or Homily) of Theophilus* (Arabic).
Dayr al-Muharraq, Nr. 12/24, fol. 1r-21v (unpublished).

TA2 = *Vision (or Homily) of Theophilus* (Arabic).
Kitab mayamir wa 'aja'ib al-'adhrâ', Second ed. (Cairo: 'Ayn Shams Press, 1927), 81–106.

Z = *Homily of Zacharias* (Arabic).
Coptic Museum, Hist. 477 (4), fol. 214r-230r (unpublished).

Z1 = *Homily of Zacharias* (Arabic).
Kitab mayamir wa 'aja'ib al-'adhrâ', Second ed. (Cairo: 'Ayn Shams Press, 1927), 56–81.

Table 2: Historical and Liturgical Works

HP	CM	Ps	SA	SE
Tell Basta	Tell Basta	Nimeshoti	Tell Basta	Tell Basta
	al-Mahamma	(Lower Egypt)		
Minyat Tanah	Minyat Tana		Samannud	Samannud
(= Bikha Isous)	(= Bikha Isous)		Bikha Isous	[Bi]kha Isous
Samnusa	Samnusa			
			Gabal al-Natrun	Gabal al-Natrun
	Minyat al-Surd			
	al-Mahamma			
	Matariya			Matariya
	(= Heliopolis)			(= Heliopolis)
	(= 'Ayn Shams)			(= 'Ayn Shams)
	Harat al-Rum			
Old Cairo		Old Cairo		
	al-Martuti			
	(= al-'Adawiya)			
Paisus	Paisus	al-Bahnasa		Paisus
	(= al-Bahnasa)	(= Paisus)		
Gabal al-Kaff	Gabal al-Kaff			
al-Ashmunayn	al-Ashmunayn	al-Ashmunayn	al-Ashmunayn	al-Ashmunayn
Filis				
Qusqam	Qusqam	Qusqam	Qusqam	Qusqam
			Old Cairo	Old Cairo
			Matariya	Matariya
			al-Mahamma	al-Mahamma

HP = *History of the Patriarchs of the Egyptian Church*. A. Atiya, Y. 'Abd al-Masih, and O. H. E. Khs-Burmester, eds. *The History of the Patriarchs of the Egyptian Church* (Cairo: Société d'archéologie copte, 1959), 227 (Arabic text), 361 (translation).

CM = Abu al-Makarim, *Churches and Monasteries of Egypt*.
Samuel al-Suryani, ed., *Tarikh al-kana'is wa-l-adyura*, Volumes 1–2 (Cairo, 1984); cf. B. T. A. Evetts, *The Churches and Monasteries of Egypt and Some Neighbouring Countries, attributed to Abu Salih, the Armenian* (London: Oxford University Press, 1895) (= *Tarikh*, Volume 1).

Ps = *Psali Batos*.
Coptic text edited by C. Labib, 3rd ed. (Cairo 1991) 714–20; cf. O. H. E. Khs-Burmester, *Koptische Handschriften 1: Die Handschriften Fragmente der Staats- und Universitätsbibliothek Hamburg*, Teil 1 (Wiesbaden, 1975), 237, 272.

SA = Arabic *Synaxarium*.
Arabic-Jacobite Synaxarium (24 Bashons), ed. R. Basset, *Patrologia Orientalis* 16 (1922), 407–11.

SE = Ethiopian *Synaxarium*.
Ethiopian Synaxarium (24 Genbot), ed. G. Colin, *Patrologia Orientalis* 47 (1997), 316–21 (124–29).

Notes

Abbreviations Used in the Notes

CSCO = *Corpus scriptorum christianorum orientalium*, ed. I. B. Chabot *et al*. Paris: Reipublicae; Leipzig: Harrassowitz, 1903–.

GCS = *Die griechischen christlichen Schriftsteller*. Berlin: Akademie, 1897–.

NPNF = *Nicene and Post-Nicene Fathers*, ed. P. Schaff *et al*. New York: Christian Literature, 1887–94; repr. Grand Rapids: Eerdmans, 1952–56.

PL = *Patrologia Latina*, ed. J.-P. Migne. Paris, 1884–86.

SC = *Sources chrétienne*, ed. H deLubac, J. Daniélou, *et al*. Paris: Cerf, 1942–.

1 Robert Gundry, *Matthew* (Grand Rapids: William B. Eerdmanns, 1987), 33–34, 38; Donald Hagner, *Matthew 1–13* (Word Biblical Commentary 33A; Dallas: Word Books, 1993), 34.

2 Raymond Brown, *The Birth of the Messiah* (Garden City, NY: Image, 1979), 544–45; Ulrich Luz, *Matthew 1–7*, trans. W. Louss (Minneapolis: Augsburg, 1989), 144–45.

3 Krister Stendahl, "Quis et Unde? An Analysis of Matthew 1–2," in *The Interpretation of Matthew*, ed. Graham Stanton (Philadelphia: Fortress, 1983), 57–58; David Garland, *Reading Matthew* (London: SPCK, 1993), 30; Brown, *The Birth of the Messiah*, 203.

4 *Commentary on Matthew 24,22*; ed. Hans Achelis, *GCS* 1.2 (1897), 201.23–29. Use of Hippolytus as a source for the Holy Family tradition is complicated by textual problems. The passage I have quoted appears in the Ethiopic version of the text, but not in the Arabic fragments. As a result, it is possible that the mention of the Holy Family's stay in Egypt was added by a later Ethiopian scribe. However, the fragmentary state of the Arabic text and the lack of other surviving manuscripts for comparison make this issue difficult to resolve. The Ethiopic text actually reads "three years and *seven* months" (201.27–28), but, considering the context, the editor has determined that "seven" is a scribal error. Instead, the text should read "three years and *six* months." This is the reason I use brackets around the word "six" in the translation I provide. Here, given the unavailability of the Ethiopic text, my translation is made from Achelis' German edition. Unless otherwise noted, all translations in this chapter will be my own and made from the original languages of the ancient sources.

5 Johannes Quasten, *Patrology*, Vol. 2 (Westminster, MD: Christian Classics, 1992), 163–64.

6 There are some variations in later, medieval sources—for instance, a twelfth-century work falsely attributed to Strabo claims the flight of the Holy Family lasted seven years (*Glossa Ordinaria* [PL 114.78]; Luz, *Matthew 1–7*, 150). A fourteenth-century Muslim commentator maintains that Jesus was in Egypt until age twelve (Ibn Kathir, Isma'il ibn 'Umar Abu al-Fida, *Qisas al-anbiya'*; ed. Mustafa Abd al-Wahid [Cairo: Dar al-kutub al-haditha, 1968], 2.411–12; Barbara F. Stowasser, *Women in the Qur'an, Traditions and Interpretation* [New York/Oxford: Oxford University Press, 1994], 75).

7 Origen, *Against Celsus* 1.28; ed. Marcel Borret, *SC* 132, 136, 147, 150 (1967–69). Celsus' writing does not survive independently; however, about ninety percent of it is preserved in Origen of Alexandria's treatise *Against Celsus*.

8 *b.Shabb.* 104b and *b.Sanh.* 107b; ed. and trans. Isidore Epstein, *The Babylonian Talmud* (London: Soncino Press, 1935, 1938).

9 The accusation that Jesus was a poor day laborer in Egypt was probably another means by which Celsus meant to disgrace his memory.

10 Origen, *Against Celsus*, 1.38; cf. 1.28.

11 Eusebius, *Proof of the Gospel*, ed. I. A. Heikel, *GCS* 23 (1913).

12 J. Quasten, *Patrology*, Vol. 3, 310. See below for early traditions concerning the Holy Family in the Thebaid (e.g., Hermopolis and Qusqam).

13 Peter Grossmann and Hans-Georg Severin, "Ashmûnayn, al-," *Coptic Encyclopedia*, 285–88; Stefan Timm, *Das christlich-koptische Ägypten in arabischer Zeit*, Vol. 1 (Wiesbaden: Dr. Ludwig Reichert, 1984), 198.

14 Gawdat Gabra, "Über die Flucht der heiligen Familie nach koptischen Traditionen," *Bulletin de Société d'archéologie copte* 38 (1999), 40.

15 *History of the Monks in Egypt* 8.1–8, ed. A. J. Festugière (Brussels: Société des Bollandistes, 1971), 41.

16 Abu al-Makarim, *Churches and Monasteries of Egypt*, fol. 77a; ed. Samuel al-Suryani, *Tarikh al-kana'is wa-l-adyura*, Vol. 2 (Cairo, 1984), 141–42; trans. B. T. Evetts, *The Churches and Monasteries of Egypt*, 221; cf. S. Timm, *Das christliche-koptische Ägypten in arabischen Zeit*, Vol. 1 (Wiesbaden: Dr. Ludwig Reichert, 1984), 208–9. The original attribution of the work to Abu Salih is false (Aziz Atiya, "Abû al-Makârim," *Coptic Encyclopedia* 23); it was in fact compiled in three or four stages by several editors, of whom Abu al-Makarim is the best known. On problems related to the authorship of this work, see Johannes den Heijer, "The Composition of the History of the Churches and Monasteries of Egypt: Some Preliminary Remarks," in *Acts of the Fifth International Congress of Coptic Studies* 2.1, ed. D. W. Johnson (Rome: C. I. M., 1993) 209–19; also Ugo Zanetti, "Abu al-Makarim et Abu Salih." *Bulletin de la Société d'archéologie copte* 34 (1995) 86–138.

17 Sozomen, *History of the Church* 5.21.8–11, ed. J. Bidez and G.C. Hansen, *GCS* 50 (1960), 229; trans. C. D. Hartranft, *NPNF*, Second Series, Vol. II (New York: Christian Literature Company, 1890), 343 (slightly modified).

18 Such was still the case in the twelfth century: an Arabic historian of that period reports that pilgrims could see a "Syrian tree" bearing red fruit—the one that had "bowed its head in adoration" at Jesus' passing—"near the ancient temple" in al-Ashmunayn (Abu al-Makarim, *Churches and Monasteries of Egypt*, fol. 77a; ed. al-Suryani, *Tarikh al-kana'is wa-l-adyura*, Vol. 2, 141–42; trans. B. T. Evetts, *The Churches and Monasteries of Egypt*, 221).

19 See, e.g., Gary Vikan, *Byzantine Pilgrimage Art* (Washington: Dumbarton Oaks, 1982).

20 E. D. Hunt, *Holy Land Pilgrimage in the Later Roman Empire, A.D. 312–460* (Oxford: Clarendon Press, 1982), esp. 83–87, 94–99; Blake Leyerle, "Landscape as Cartography in Early Christian Pilgrimage Narratives," *Journal of the American Academy of Religion* 64.1 (1996), 119–43.

21 For a discussion of the role of landscape in the context of Egyptian pilgrimage, see David Frankfurter, "Introduction," in *Pilgrimage and Holy Space in Late Antique Egypt* (Leiden: Brill, 1998), 16–18, 24.

22 Besa, *Life of Shenoute* 157; ed. I. Leipoldt and W. E. Crum, *CSCO* 1, Scriptores Coptici, Series Secunda, Tomus II (Lipsius: Otto Harrossowitz, 1906), 67.28—68.1; trans. David N. Bell, *The Life of Shenoute* (Cistercian Studies Series 73; Kalamazoo: Cistercian Publications, 1983), 85–86.

23 Other Coptic sources from this period report similar revelations given to Egyptian martyrs and bishops about the Holy Family's visit to Hermopolis. For example, in the Coptic *Martyrdom of Apater and Irai*, Jesus appears to one of the martyrs and identifies Shmoun (Hermopolis/al-Ashmunayn) as the place "where I received hospitality with Mary, my mother, and Joseph" (ed. H. Hyvernat, *Les actes des martyrs de l'Égypte tirés des manuscrits coptes de la Bibliothéque Vaticane et du Musée Borgia* [Paris: Ernest Leroux, 1886], 92.4–5 [f. 64]). This work is preserved in an eighth- or ninth-century Coptic manuscript (no. 73) in the Vatican Library (R. P. Michel Jullien, "Traditions et légendes coptes sur le voyage de la sainte-famille en Égypte," *Les Missions Catholiques* 19 [1887], 10). In the Coptic *Martyrdom of Paese and*

Thecla (69Vi), the Virgin Mary appears to the martyr Thecla and tells her, "I was dwelling in the city of Shmoun, I and my little Son feeding at my breast" (ed. and trans. E. A. E. Reymond and J. W. B. Barns, *Four Martyrdoms from the Pierpont Morgan Coptic Codices* [Oxford: Clarendon Press, 1973] 57, 167; W. Till, *Koptische Heiligen- und Märtyrerlegenden*, Bd. 1, Teil 1 [Orientalia Christiana Analecta 102; Rome, 1935] 80, 91). The Coptic text edited by Reymond and Barns dates to the ninth century, but the earliest reference to the story of Paese and Thecla appears in a Greek papyrus from the fifth or early sixth century (*P.Berl.Sarisch.* 3). A vision of the Virgin Mary also plays a central role in various versions of a later homily attributed to the Alexandrian patriarch Theophilus (I discuss this source in greater detail below).

24 *Gospel of Pseudo-Matthew* 22–24; ed. P. Peeters, *Évangiles apocryphes*, Vol. 1 (Paris: Auguste Picard, 1924), 121–24; trans. O. Cullman, in *New Testament Apocrypha*, Vol. 1, ed. W. Schneemelcher and R. McL. Wilson (Cambridge: James Clarke & Co., 1991), 464. The dating of this work is uncertain: Cullman (*New Testament Apocrypha*, Vol. 1, 458) conjectures that it was written in the eighth or ninth century. However, some of the oral traditions behind this *Gospel* probably date even earlier.

25 *Gospel of Pseudo-Matthew* 20–21; ed. P. Peeters, *Évangiles apocryphes*, Vol. 1, 116–20; trans. O. Cullman, in *New Testament Apocrypha*, Vol. 1, 463–64.

26 Quran, Sura 19.22–26; trans. M. Pickthall, *The Meaning of the Glorious Qur'an* (Beirut: Dar al-Kitab al-Lubnani, 1970), 397; see also A. J. Wensinck, "Maryam," in *The Encyclopedia of Islam*, New edition, Vol. 6, ed. C. E. Bosworth et al. (Leiden: E. J. Brill, 1989), 631.

27 Al-Maqrizi, *Topography and History of Egypt* 9; in *Mémoires de la Mission archéologique français du Cairo*, Tome 16, Fasc. 1 (Paris: Ernest Leroux, 1895/1906), 74.

28 On early Holy Family tradition in Qusqam, see Leslie B. MacCoull, "The Holy Family Pilgrimage in Late Antique Egypt: The Case of Qosqam," in *Akten des XII internationalen Kongresses für christliche Archäologie: Bonn 22.–28. September, 1991*, ed. E. Dassmann and J. Engemann (Jahrbuch für Antike und Christentum, Ergänzungsband 20; Münster: Aschendorffsche Verlagsbuchhandlung, 1995–97), 987–93; S. Timm, *Das christlich-koptische Ägypten in arabischer Zeit*, Vol. 5, 2,180–91.

29 The *Vision of Theophilus* was originally written in Coptic; however the full text currently survives only in Arabic, Syriac, and Ethiopic translations, none dating earlier than the fourteenth century. The Syriac translation seems to predate the surviving Arabic and Ethiopic texts. As a result, in this book I will cite this version most often. The Syriac text is edited and translated by Alphonse Mingana, "Vision of Theophilus, or the Book of the Flight of the Holy Family into Egypt," *Woodbrooke Studies* 3.1 (Cambridge: W. Heffer & Sons, 1931), 1–43 (English translation), 44–92 (Syriac text); cf. François Nau, "La version syriaque de la Vision de Théophile dur le séjour de la vierge en Égypte," *Revue de l'Orient Chrétien* 15 (1910), 125–32. For Arabic versions of the text, see Massimo Guidi, "La omelia di Teofilo di Alessandria sul monte Coscam nelle letterature orientale," in *Rendiconti della Reale Accademia Nazionale dei Lincei*, Serie V, Classe di scienze storiche 26 (1917), 381–91, 441–69 (text); *Kitab mayamir wa 'aja'ib al-'adhrâ'*, Second edition (Cairo: 'Ayn Shams Press, 1927), 81–106; cf. Georg Graf, *Geschichte der christlichen arabischen Literatur*, Vol. 1 (Studi e Testi 118; Città del Vaticano: Bibliotheca Apostolica Vaticana, 1944), 229–32. The Arabic text has undergone successive redactions and expansions (see appendix; also Gawdat Gabra, "Über die Flucht der heiligen Familie," 43–44). For the Ethiopic version, see E. A. Wallis Budge, *Legends of Our Lady Mary the Perpetual Virgin and her Mother Hanna* (London: Oxford University Press, 1933), 61–80. At the time of writing, Anne Boud'hors and Ramez Wadie Boutros were editing a Coptic fragment of this text preserved in the Bibliothèque Nationale in Paris, to be published in the series *Patrologia Orientalis*.

30 Mingana, "Vision," 42. Compare this to the entry on 6 Hatur in René Basset, ed., "Le synaxaire arabe jacobite," cf. the Arabic-Jacobite Synaxarium (6 Hathur), ed. René Basset, *Patrologia Orientalis* 3:255.

31 Otto Meinardus (*Monks and Monasteries of the Egyptian Deserts*, rev. ed. [Cairo: American University in Cairo Press, 1992], 158) suggests that this sermon may have been preached right after the restoration of the monastic church in the twelfth century. This time frame approximately corresponds to the view of Mingana ("Vision," 3–8), who believes that the work was originally written in Arabic around the eleventh (or twelfth) century. Leslie MacCoull ("Holy Family Pilgrimage in Late Antique Egypt," 988) believes the tradition at Qusqam originated earlier, giving the eighth century as an early estimate.

32 Mingana, "Vision," 10–12.

33 Mingana, "Vision," 21–22, 24–26.

34 On the borrowing and adaptation of legends as a form of cultic competition, see Stephen Davis, "Pilgrimage and the Cult of Saint Thecla in Late Antique Egypt," in *Pilgrimage and Holy Space in Late Antique Egypt*, ed. David Frankfurter (Leiden: Brill, 1998), 303–39, esp. 317–23. A revised version of this article will appear as chapter four in my forthcoming book, *The Cult of Saint Thecla* (Oxford: Oxford University Press, 2001).

35 Mingana, "Vision," 26–29. The Arabic Infancy Gospel may preserve an earlier version of this legend about two thieves. In that source, the two thieves are named (Titus and Dumachus), but the place where they encounter the Holy Family is not Qusqam. A later version of this legend appears in a homily attributed to "Timothy, patriarch of Alexandria" (probably Timothy Aelurus, 457–77). However, this attribution is false; the homily was originally composed by a later Coptic writer. A thirteenth-century Coptic fragment of the work is preserved in Paris (Paris MS. Copte 131^5; L. MacCoull, "Holy Family Pilgrimage in Late Antique Egypt," 988, 990–91). A later Ethiopic version also exists (Budge, *Legends of Our Lady Mary the Perpetual Virgin and her Mother Hanna*, 81–101). In any case, this work attributed to Timothy had to be composed sometime after the *Vision of Theophilus*, because the author knows and refers to that work (Paris MS. Copte 131^5, fol. 103r; *Narrative of the Virgin Mary* 18 [ed. Budge, *Legends*, 100]).

36 Mingana, "Vision," 36, cf. 29–30.

37 Mingana, "Vision," 31–34; cf. G. Graf, *Geschichte der christlichen arabischen Literatur*, Vol. 1, 230.

38 For recent studies that discuss paired saints, see Virgil S. Crisafulli and John W. Nesbitt, *The Miracles of St. Artemios: A Collection of Miracle Stories by an Anonymous Author of Seventh-Century Byzantium* (Leiden: E. J. Brill, 1997), esp. 13–14; Dominic Montserrat, "Pilgrimage to the Shrine of SS Cyrus and John at Menouthis in Late Antiquity," in *Pilgrimage and Holy Space in Late Antique Egypt*, ed. David Frankfurter (Leiden: Brill, 1998), 257–79; and Stephen Davis, "Pilgrimage and the Cult of Saint Thecla in Late Antique Egypt," 303–39.

39 Mingana, "Vision," 37–39.

40 The story of this post-Resurrection visit contains references to liturgical artifacts established by Jesus and his apostles: a vessel containing water for consecration, vestments, and ritual of the mass (Mingana, "Vision," 38–39). At the medieval Dayr al-Muharraq, such objects were probably displayed for pilgrims as tangible 'evidence' of the Savior's second visit.

41 Abu al-Makarim, *Churches and Monasteries of Egypt*, fol. 75b–76a, 86a–b; ed. al-Suryani, *Tarikh al-kana'is wa-l-adyura*, Vol. 2, 139–40, 160; trans. B. T. Evetts, *The Churches and Monasteries of Egypt*, 217–19, 233–34. The Holy Family's visit to Gabal al-Kaff is also mentioned in a twelfth-century redaction of the *History of the Patriarchs of the Egyptian Church*, ed. Atiya et al., 227 (Arabic text), 361 (trans-

lation). On the redaction of this work, see two articles by Johannes den Heijer: "Mawhub Ibn Mansur Ibn Mufarrig et l'historiographie Copto-Arabe," *CSCO* 513 (Louvain, 1989), 217–20; and "History of the Patriarchs of Alexandria," *Coptic Encyclopedia*, 1,238–42.

42 A similar legend is recorded in the *Vision of Theophilus*: although Gabal al-Kaff is not explicitly named, the geography in the narrative seems to correspond with the location of this site (Mingana, "Vision," 21). A later Arabic version of this homily explicitly includes the name Gabal al-Kaff in its itinerary of the Holy Family (MS 12/24 from Dayr al-Muharraq, fol. 7v–11r; Gawdat Gabra, "Über die Flucht der heiligen Familie," 43.

43 Abu al-Makarim, *Churches and Monasteries of Egypt*, fol. 86a–b; ed. Samuel al-Suriani, *Tarikh al-kana'is wa-l-adyura*, Vol. 2, 160; trans. B. T. Evetts, *The Churches and Monasteries of Egypt*, 234–44.

44 Abu al-Makarim, *Churches and Monasteries of Egypt*, fol. 76a–b; ed. al-Suryani, *Tarikh al-kana'is wa-l-adyura*, Vol. 2, 140–41; trans. B. T. Evetts, *The Churches and Monasteries of Egypt*, 219–20; *History of the Patriarchs of the Egyptian Church*, ed. Atiya et al., 227 (Arabic text), 361 (translation). Other later sources include the liturgical texts *Psali Batos* (which mentions only al-Bahnasa), the *Psali Adam*, and the Ethiopian Synaxarium (Youhanna N. Youssef, "Notes on the Traditions Concerning the Flight of the Holy Family into Egypt," *Coptic Church Review* 20.2 [1999], 48–55). The Coptic texts of the *Psali Batos* and the *Psali Adam* have been edited by C. Labib (3rd ed.; Cairo, 1991), 714–25. For the Ethiopian Synaxarium (24 Genbot), see the text edited by G. Colin, *Patrologia Orientalis* 47 (1997), 316–21.

45 The fifteenth-century historian al-Maqrizi also mentions this well in his *Topography and History of Egypt* (trans. B. T. Evetts, *Churches and Monasteries of Egypt*, Appendix, 313).

46 Cyriacus, *Homily on the Visit of the Blessed Virgin and her Beloved Son at the Holy Monastery now known as Pai Isus or the House of Jesus in the City of al-Bahnasa*; *Kitab mayamir wa 'aja'ib al-'adhrâ'*, Second ed. (Cairo: 'Ayn Shams Press, 1927), 119–39. A second homily attributed to Cyriacus in the same edition is actually a plagiarized version of the first (*Kitab mayamir*, 106–118; G. Graf, *Geschichte der christlichen arabischen Literatur*, Vol. 1, 232–34). For a summary of these two texts, see Pierre Dib, "Deux discours de Cyriaque, évêque de Behnésa sur la fuite en Égypt," *Revue de l'Orient chrétien* 15 (1910), 157–61.

47 For a discussion of Cyriacus, see also R.G. Coquin, "Cyriacus," *Coptic Encyclopedia*, 669–71.

48 G. Graf, *Geschichte der christlichen arabischen Literatur*, 232–33.

49 In another sermon attributed to Cyriacus—which borrows heavily from the first one—the Holy Family tradition at al-Bahnasa is explicitly linked with the more well-known traditions at Qusqam. The author of this work was probably a later monk from Dayr al-Muharraq who modified the earlier sermon to include traditions from that monastery (*Kitab mayamir wa 'aja'ib al-'adhrâ'*, 106–18; G. Graf, *Geschichte der christlichen arabischen Literatur*, 233–34).

50 *Kitab mayamir wa 'aja'ib al-'adhrâ'*, 135–36. Here, the writer presents the monastery as the fulfillment of Jesus' ministry in the Gospels (Matt. 11:5 and 15:30; cf. Luke 7:22). A similar exegesis of Matthew is attested much earlier in relation to the Holy Family tradition at al-Ashmunayn (Besa, *Life of Shenoute* 157; ed. I. Leipoldt and W. E. Crum, *CSCO* 1, Scriptores Coptici, Series Secunda, Tomus II, 68.2–5; David N. Bell, *The Life of Shenoute*, Cistercian Studies Series 73 (Kalamazoo: Cistercian Publications, 1983), 86.

51 Meinardus (*The Holy Family in Egypt*, 44–47) reports on several Muslim traditions related to the Holy Family at al-Bahnasa. However, his citation of dates and sources is not clear.

52 *Itinerarium Antonini Placentini*; ed. C. Milani, *Itinerarium Antonini Placentini: Un viaggio in Terra Santa del 560–570 d.C.* (Milan, 1977). An English translation is available in John Wilkinson, *Jerusalem Pilgrims Before the Crusades* (Warminster: Aris & Phillips, 1977), 77ff.; also Antoninus Martyr, "Of the Holy Land Visited," in *Palestine Pilgrim Text Society* II (London, 1896). In some sources, this pilgrim from Piacenza also goes by the name Antoninus of Placentia.

53 Cited by Meinardus, *The Holy Family in Egypt*, 63.

54 Pelusium was home to the early fifth-century monk Isidore (d. ca. A.D. 435), whose surviving writings include around 2,000 letters (Quasten, *Patrology*, Vol. 3, 180–85).

55 Meinardus, *The Holy Family in Egypt*, 26. The family's stop at Farama is only briefly mentioned in a late version of a homily attributed to Bishop Zacharias of Sakha (*Kitab mayamir wa 'aja'ib al-'adhrâ'*, 68).

56 Mingana, "Vision," 19–21, cf. 26. In another version of this story attributed to Zacharias of Sakha, Joseph digs under the tree until the spring appears (*Kitab mayamir wa 'aja'ib al-'adhrâ'*, 68–69).

57 *Narrative of the Virgin Mary* 12; ed. and trans. E. A. W. Budge, *Legends of Our Lady Mary the Perpetual Virgin and her Mother Hanna*, 86–87. The Ethiopic version of this text preserves traditions from that country, and was undoubtedly redacted by a later Ethiopian author. The manuscript of this text is preserved in the British Museum (MS Orient. No. 604, fol. 256ff.) and dates to the eighteenth century A.D., although it was copied from an older manuscript (Budge, *Legends*, lxxi). An earlier Coptic version of this text is also extant (Paris MS. Copte 131⁵; L. MacCoull, "Holy Family Pilgrimage in Late Antique Egypt," 988, 990–91).

58 For an example of this image on a Coptic icon, see *The Escape to Egypt according to Coptic Tradition* (Cairo: Lehnert & Landrock, 1993), 44, cf. 51.

59 Abu al-Makarim, *Churches and Monasteries of Egypt* 44b–45b; ed. al-Suryani, *Tarikh al-kana'is wa-l-adyura*, Vol. 1, 70–71; Arabic-Jacobite Synaxarium (24 Bashons), ed. Basset, 408–9.

60 *The Holy Family in Egypt*, Egyptian Ministry of Tourism (Cairo: United Printing and Publishing Co., 1999), 22–23.

61 C. Detlef G. Müller, "Zacharias, Saint," *Coptic Encyclopedia*, 2,368–69.

62 Y. N. Youssef, "Notes on the Traditions Concerning the Flight of the Holy Family into Egypt," *Coptic Church Review* 20.2 (1999), 48–55; *contra* G. Graf, *Geschichte der christlichen arabischen Literatur*, 227–29. While Graf thinks Zacharias wrote the homily, he admits that the work exhibits marked stylistic differences from his other known works. On the homily's dependence on the *Vision of Theophilus*, see G. Gabra, "Über die Flucht der heiligen Familie," 43ff.

63 Here I use the earliest available text traditions for each work. For the *Vision of Theophilus*, see the text edited by Alphonse Mingana in *Woodbrooke Studies* 3.1 (Cambridge: W. Heffer & Sons, 1931), 1–43, 44–92. For the *Homily of Zacharias*, I refer to a manuscript in the Coptic Museum: Hist. 477 (4), fol. 214f–230r); Marcus Simaika, *Catalogue of the Coptic and Arabic Manuscripts in the Coptic Museum, the Patriarchate, the Principal Churches of Cairo and Alexandria and the Monasteries of Egypt*, Vol. 1 (Cairo, 1939), 56, ser. no. 105, Hist. 477; cited by G. Gabra, "Über die Flucht der heiligen Familie," 43. These texts are labeled Tˢ and Z respectively in the appendix.

64 *Kitab mayamir wa 'aja'ib al-'adhrâ'*, 56–81, esp. 71.

65 *Arabic Infancy Gospel* 24; ed. P. Peeters, *Évangiles apocryphes* I, 28; Arabic-Jacobite Synaxarium (24 Bashons), ed. Basset, 409; Ethiopian Synaxarium (24 Genbot), ed. G. Colin, in *Patrologia Orientalis* 47 (1997), 316–21 (124–29).

66 Meinardus, *The Holy Family in Egypt*, 38–39.

67 For these travel accounts, see Burchard of Mount Sion, "Description of the Holy Land," in *Palestine Pilgrims' Text Society* 12 (Repr.; New York: AMS Press,

1971); and Pero Tafur, *Travels and Adventures* (London: George Routledge & Sons, 1926).

68 Marino Sanuto, "Secrets for True Crusaders," in *Palestine Pilgrims' Text Society* 12 (Repr.; New York: AMS Press, 1971).

69 For a description of the guardians at Matariya, see Ludolph von Suchem, "Description of the Holy Land," in *Palestine Pilgrims' Text Society* 12 (Repr.; New York: AMS Press, 1971).

70 Felix Fabri, *Voyage en Égypte*, ed. and trans. J. Masson (Cairo: Institut français orientale du Caire, 1975).

71 Arabic-Jacobite Synaxarium (24 Bashons), ed. R. Basset, 409. For the text from the *Difnar* on the Holy Family, including this tradition about Abu Sarga, see G. Gabra, "Über die Flucht der heiligen Familie," 45–48.

72 Abu al-Makarim, *Churches and Monasteries of Egypt*, fol. 44a–45a; ed. al-Suryani, *Tarikh al-kana'is wa-l-adyura*, Vol. 2, 78–83; trans. B. T. Evetts, *The Churches and Monasteries of Egypt*, 136–41.

73 For contrasting opinions on the location of the Church of al-Martuti at al-'Adawiyah, see B. T. Evetts, ed., *The Churches and Monasteries of Egypt*, 136–37, notes 4 and 5; and Nabih Kamil Dawud, *Tarikh kanisat al-sayyida al-'adhrâ' bil-Ma'adi* (Cairo, 1999), 11–18. Dawud cites a number of medieval Arabic sources that mention the church (and monastery) of al-'Adawiya. However, his earliest source that explicitly connects the Church of al-'Adawiya with Ma'adi dates from the late eighteenth century.

74 Abu al-Makarim, *Churches and Monasteries of Egypt*, fol. 44a–b; trans. B.T. Evetts, *The Churches and Monasteries of Egypt*, 137.

The Holy Family in Egypt

Sites the Holy Family are believed to have visited are indicated by italic type

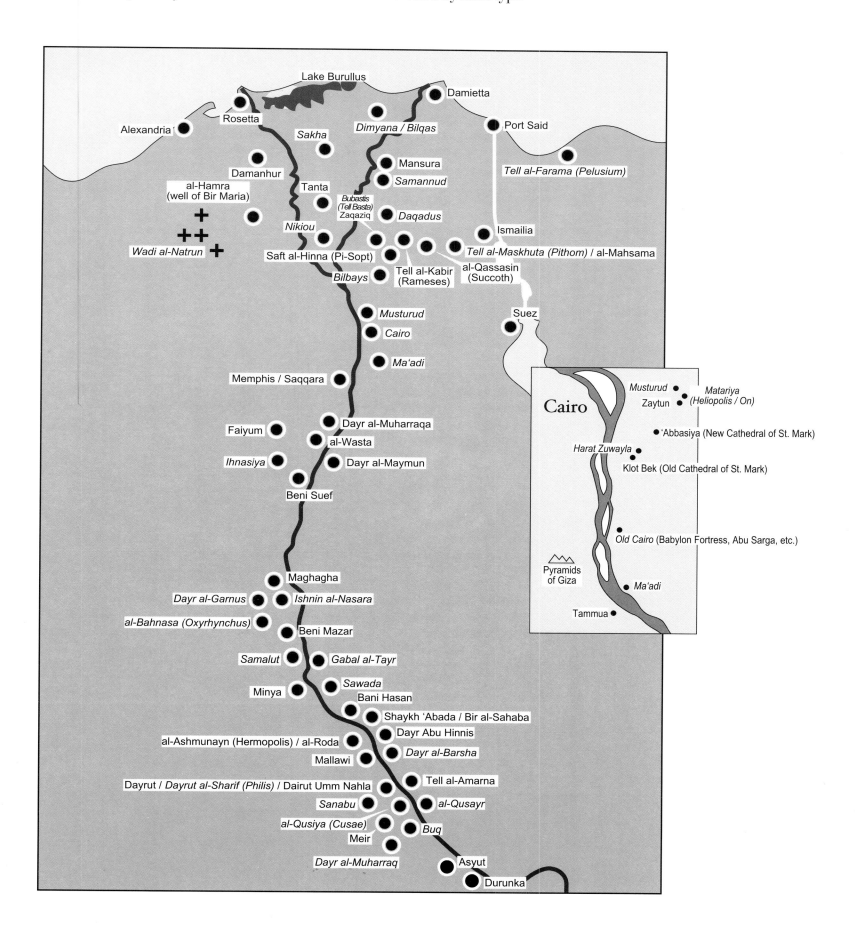

The National Egyptian Heritage Revival Association (NEHRA)

A message from Mounir Ghabbour, Chairman

To ensure the continued existence of Egypt's valuable monuments, which represent one of the most important attractions to visitors to Egypt, and to participate in the tremendous efforts exerted by the Egyptian government, the National Egyptian Heritage Revival Association (NEHRA) was established with the encouragement of President Mohamed Hosni Mubarak and with the cooperation of the Ministries of Tourism, Culture, and Environment.

The goals and work plans of NEHRA are as follows:
- to restore sites on the route of the Holy Family
- to upgrade the environment of historic sites of religious importance
- to help Egyptian and international tourism companies market these sites
- to promote historical and cultural awareness of the ancient Egyptian heritage
- to have the sites registered by UNESCO

In Phase I of the project, the following sites in Cairo have been restored:
- the Monastery and Tomb of Saint Dimyana
- 86 icons and the cross of the Church of the Holy Virgin in Harat Zuwayla
- the crypt and icons of the Church of the Holy Virgin at Musturud
- the well and tree of the Holy Virgin at Matariya
- the Crypt of the Holy Family at the Church of the Holy Virgin at Ma'adi

In Phase II, the following additional sites in Cairo, all currently flooded by sewage water, will be restored:
- the Church of the Holy Virgin in Harat Zuwayla
- the Crypt of the Holy Family at the Church of Abu Sarga
- the Sabil of Sharif Tabataba

In Phase III, the following sites outside Cairo will be restored:
- Farma (North Sinai), the site of six buried churches
- the churches and monasteries of Upper Egypt
- Gabal al-Tayr and Ishnin al-Nasara
- Dayr al-Garnus and Dayr al-Muharraq

The National Egyptian Heritage Revival Association (NEHRA)
19 El Badw Street, Heliopolis, Cairo
Tel: 0020-2-2435277, Fax: 0020-2-2639615/644-2344

Church of the Holy Virgin at Gabal al-Tayr